earthly Fathers

a memoir

earthly Fathers

a memoir

A coming-of-age story about faith
and the search for a father's love

Scott Sawyer

ZondervanPublishingHouse
Grand Rapids, Michigan

A Division of HarperCollins*Publishers*

Earthly Fathers
Copyright © 2001 by Scott Sawyer

Requests for information should be addressed to:

🏭 ZondervanPublishingHouse

Grand Rapids, Michigan 49530

Library of Congress Cataloging-in-Publication Data
Sawyer, Scott.
     Earthly fathers : a memoir / Scott Sawyer.
          p.   cm.
     ISBN 0-310-23003-9
     1. Sawyer, Scott.   2. Fathers and sons—Texas.   3. Spiritual biography.
4. Texas—Biography.   I. Title.

CT275.S3389 A3 2001
976.4'063'092–dc21
[B]
                                                                00–051290

This edition is printed on acid-free paper.

Interior design by Melissa Elenbaas

Printed in the United States of America

01 02 03 04 05 /❖ DC/ 10 9 8 7 6 5 4 3 2 1

Contents

For my wife, Joy,

and for my family

Posterity will serve him;

future generations will be told about the Lord,

and proclaim his deliverance to a people yet unborn,

saying that he has done it.

—Psalm 22:30–31 NRSV

Part I

one

Names

1

HE WASN'T OUR REAL FATHER. HE WAS DADDY ROBERT. THE one who had a last name different from ours.

Charles Robert Sawyer.

Daddy Robert—the father who looked different from us. Whose face wasn't like ours. His was round—ours were long. And he wasn't skinny, as we were. He was tall, but stocky and strong. When my big brother, Tommy, and I asked him to flex his muscles for us, he usually demurred. But when he complied, his biceps became like boulders. Tommy and I each wrapped our tightest grip around an arm, and, in one swoop, he lifted us both off the ground.

Daddy Robert didn't talk to us the way our mother did. And he didn't touch us the way Momma did. He was hard to Momma's soft, no to her yes. He smoked Kools, in the green package, not Momma's red Winstons. And he blew the smoke out through his nose, like a dragon, not just out of his mouth the way Momma did.

He wasn't the father in our baby photos—the father who held us, jiggled us, gave us nicknames to go with the first traits we showed. He hadn't been there then.

Yet Daddy Robert *was* our father. He'd been with us from the time *we* could remember. He was the father we knew—the one we touched, saw, tasted, smelled. The one we examined as he napped on Saturday afternoons—his stomach rising and falling, his twisty gold watchband stretched around his thick, hairy wrist, his black-framed glasses tucked neatly between his ears and brown hair. Everything rising and falling, rising and falling.

He was the father whose few waking words amused us, scared us, taught us to pay attention, doubled us over in laughter as no one else could. Whose work—along with our mother's—gave us allowance, school clothes, even cars when we graduated. Whose every expression, tender or loud, loving or profane, increased his mystery to us.

He rarely divulged his own youth to us. But he took us to the elementary school field to hit pop flies to us, so we could break in our gloves before our first year of Little League. He punted high ones to us at the old high school football field—the one where his knee had been hurt, years before—so we could practice catching and see how it felt to be out there. He was the father who seemed to love us, but who at times seemed apart from us and alone.

Our real father was Daddy Ronnie.

Ronnie Witten Burk.

The father who had died before we knew him. The one who'd swept Momma off her feet in college. A tall, lanky senior who walked into the lobby of her dorm and recognized the blonde freshman, even though it was a blind date. Her back was turned to him, yet somehow he knew this was Patricia Meadows. He checked his cool, strode up behind her, and said, "Hi, Patty Pigtails." And that was that.

He was the father who, as a first-year coach in the small town of West, Texas, had set his sights on becoming head track coach

reclining, greeting people with magnanimity. Being curious and inquiring with acquaintances, yet vaguely distant. Friendly and well-met on some days, moody and retreating on others.

It's why I have the familiar traits of the earthly father I *did* witness—the way I jest when I'm ill at ease, deflect compliments, tease with unearned familiarity—a familiarity meant to usher in an informal bond but that actually establishes distance.

It's why I have the brooding thoughts of one father, the practical worries of the other. The gracious humor of one, the earthy, bawdy perspective of the other. The pretension to other-worldly nobility of one, the lip-biting stoicism of the other.

Maybe it's why. Or maybe it's not.

But Daddy Robert *was* perfect, we thought. Because he *was* our father.

I looked at his picture next to Momma's on the wall in their bedroom and saw a perfect man—handsome, muscular, youthful. How was he any less perfect than Daddy Ronnie? Both had dark hair—not like Momma, whose hair was blonde. Both were tall and strong, in contrast to Momma's softness and tenderness. Both were larger than life to us, larger even than our imaginations allowed. The way all fathers are.

Daddy Robert—our father with us. *Robert Sawyer.* The insurance man, not the coach. The city man, not the farm boy. The father who went dove hunting one Saturday each year, not the father who wanted to go fishing every weekend. The Deke, not the Sig Ep. The University of Texas dropout, not the North Texas State grad. The powerful running back, not the lanky split end. The one who'd twisted his knee on a high school football field and was never the same. Not the one who went to college on a track scholarship.

He was Daddy Robert—the second one, not the first one.

Daddy Robert wasn't the one who might have raised us on a farm in keeping with family tradition. Who might have taught us to fish in a stock tank, grow vegetables, milk cows, kill rattle-snakes. Who might have disciplined us with stern authority. Who might have.

Instead, Daddy Robert was the one who came home at night from his insurance job in Dallas. He brought home bags of Sonic burgers or Pizza Hut boxes on weeknights when Momma stayed late at the high school for her drama students' play practices. He mowed the lawn and washed the car on weekends. He spanked Tommy for getting bad grades in conduct. He got irritated at us, threw footballs to us in the front yard, fried an occasional dinner, laughed with Momma, got in arguments with her, stayed up late on Christmas Eve setting up our toys. He scared us into laughter, when we turned off all the lights in the house and had to find him, and he'd pop up out of nowhere shining a flashlight underneath his face, having covered it with Momma's pantyhose. He scared us for real at times.

At times he pounded his fist on the kitchen table when one of us spilled something. At times he let out a string of curse words whenever something went awry. He couldn't hide his frustration whenever we did something wrong that we didn't know was wrong. And he couldn't hide his contempt whenever we did something wrong and we knew it.

Daddy Ronnie—our father in heaven. Tommy and I were reminded of him every day at school, as we sang "My Country 'Tis of Thee." When we came to the line that says, "Land where our fathers died," we each started crying in our respective classrooms. Every day we were taken to the principal's office separately, and our mother was phoned at the high school.

We never talked about our sadness to each other, much less offered an explanation to anyone else. But we each knew why the other cried. We cried because *he* had died. And even though we'd never really known him, we knew his dying was sad.

Tommy was fifteen months old, I eight weeks, when Daddy Ronnie died. Our grandmother, Nanny, was a nurse, and she'd given each of us the polio vaccine—Momma, Tommy, me. But, evidently, Daddy Ronnie waited around too long, and never took his. He got sick, caught pneumonia from the complications, and died—all within two weeks.

—Why didn't he take the vaccine?
My mother hesitates. She musters a gracious smile for me. She always does when we speak of those days.
—I don't know, honey. I think he was probably working out at the time, trying to stay in shape. He was careful about his training. He never wanted to put anything in his body that might interrupt that.

But, polio?

When you're younger, you accept that kind of answer. I accepted it as a child—not because it made sense, but because it gave me something more of him. Something more to imagine about him, to lock onto. One more myth that sculpted another feature in him—dedication? pride? neglect?

Grief does odd things to people. When Daddy Ronnie died, and Tommy and I were still babies, Momma decided to go back to college to finish her degree.
Patricia Meadows Burk.
She knew she had to support us somehow. So she moved us back in with her parents, Nanny and Granddaddy, and reenrolled at North Texas State College, where she'd met Daddy Ronnie. The college was in Denton, on the far side of Dallas from my grandparents' home in Waxahachie. The drive was a

three-hour round-trip at minimum. Momma decided to room at the college during the week, and drive home on weekends to be with us.

A year later, Tommy and I stood holding Nanny's hands on a curb near the campus, waiting to greet Momma. It was a Saturday morning in the fall. We watched as a parade of uniformed college students passed by us on the street. Finally, we caught a glimpse of our mother. From around the corner chugged a long, wide homecoming float. Momma was standing on it and waving, wearing a crown on her head.

—Did we recognize you?
The briefest of moments passes. Again, she smiles.
—Nanny pointed me out to you. Tommy was old enough to recognize me, and he waved.
Her eyes are wet.
—But you were still too young. Nanny took your hand and waved it.
She lets herself cry.
She'd cried back then, too, she says. Even as she waved to everyone in the crowd.
She just hadn't known what to do, she explained.

I remember a portrait of her wearing a crown. It was a tinted photograph of faint yellow and blue, to match her blonde hair and blue-green eyes. It hung somewhere in Nanny and Granddaddy's home, and we saw it every day. Whether the crown in that photo was the same one we saw in the parade, I don't know. It easily could have been another. Granddaddy had always told my mother, "Tricia, walk in like you own the place." She took him at his word.

Yet it would have been difficult for my mother to be arrogant. Nanny wouldn't abide any favoritism in her family. For a lifelong Republican (an odd loyalty for a dirt-poor farm girl from red-clay Georgia), she was strictly democratic toward her children. Granddaddy at least gave lip service to this, and still does.

"I love you, Daddy," one of his children says.

"I love all my children," he answers slyly.

But Uncle Dennis, Momma's younger brother, tells me, "Tricia always had Daddy wrapped around her finger."

I never would have guessed it. In fact, I'd have thought the opposite. I'd known my mother to have a flaw of melancholy. She cried at night when she read to Tommy and me—books with heart-wrenching passages, such as *Black Beauty* and *Charlotte's Web*. We learned to cry along with her, even if we hadn't been listening.

Yet her melancholy made her a good listener and a consistent giver. She seemed to want to shore up others' courage in places where hers couldn't be. In some ways, she was supremely confident of the ground beneath her feet—in other ways, frightfully aware of the fragility of life.

She lay on the narrow bed in my grandparents' small guest bedroom. She'd lain there almost continually for a month.

The air was still. The afternoon sun bore through the blinds, making dust particles glow like circling vultures.

Someone entered the room.

—Tricia.

She was unable to move.

—Tricia.

It was her father.

—Oh, she said.

He pulled up a chair.

—What, Daddy.

He leaned forward, his hands folded.

—You have to get up, Tricia.

She said nothing.

—You've got to get up and do something.
She knew this. But what was there to do?
—What do you think I should do, Daddy?
—What do you want to do?
—I don't know.
She didn't.
—Have you thought about it at all?
She had imagined only a few things.
—I thought about becoming a stewardess.
Her father dropped his head.
—That's not for you, Tricia.
She turned her head to the wall. Gazed at the big square of sun-
light. It had barely moved since she last saw it.
—Why don't you go back and finish school? he said.
She didn't answer. She was thinking about her babies.
—Your mother and I can help you. I think you need to finish your
education, Tricia. Nobody can take that away from you.

We were the babies.
Tommy—*Thomas Witten Burk*.
And Scotty—*Ronnie Scott Burk*.
Everybody said Tommy looked just like Daddy Ronnie—
from the slight, downward curve of his nose to the pronounced
dimple in his chin. We checked this out for ourselves in our
baby albums. Black-and-white photos, with Momma's handwriting at the bottom of each, pasted onto black pages. There
was a picture of Tommy lying in his crib, looking up, his tiny
nose jagged even then. *That* does *look like Daddy Ronnie*. A picture of him wearing Daddy Ronnie's hunting hat. A picture of
him in diapers, trying to walk in Daddy Ronnie's work boots.
Then, a picture of Daddy Ronnie holding Tommy in one arm—
father and son staring comically at each other.
"He would toss you in the air," Granddaddy told Tommy,
"and you would *laugh* and *laugh*."

When Tommy got big enough, Nanny bought him some jeans. She cuffed the pants using white material with a red-polka-dot pattern. That Friday, when Momma came home from college in Denton and saw Tommy wearing those pants, she burst into tears. She had the same reaction later, when she walked in one weekend and heard Tommy call Nanny "Momma."

That's the day, my mother tells me, when she began racing home even faster. She regularly topped one hundred. Every week, she was stopped by one of the highway patrolmen on U.S. 77. She didn't care. She became known among them as the "wicked widow of Waxahachie." Yet those men always let her go without giving her a ticket. They'd all heard her story, at one time or another, and they believed her as she told it. Her first baby had become a little boy, she said, and she hadn't been looking.

On Saturdays, we all watched a TV program hosted by a dark-haired emcee. Every time Tommy saw this man, he pointed to the screen excitedly and said, "Daddy." He thought it was our father. Our father—somewhere out there, away from us, but somehow still near.

In later years, my big brother always claimed he remembered Daddy Ronnie. But I was never sure if he did. I always thought that maybe it was the dream of our father that appealed to Tommy—that our first father was alive somewhere, even if it was in heaven.

There's a pair of elementary school pictures of Tommy and me that, in my mind, typified us. My brother's sandy brown hair is slightly grown out from a crewcut. He's got a cowlick on one side of his forehead that would stay with him throughout his life. His head is turned slightly to one side, and you can't tell from his expression if he's being sly or just shy. Either would have been true of him. More tellingly, there's a round, slightly misshapen, blood-colored scab between his upper lip and his right nostril. How Tommy managed to get a scrape in that unlikely location may have been clear at the time, but it escapes us all now.

As for me, I'm looking straight at the camera. Careful to turn neither to the right nor left. Just doing my job, teacher—staying out of trouble, making good grades, using my extra time after assignments to draw pictures. My hair is combed neatly, my face well-scrubbed, my forehead shiny. I'm even wearing a button-down collar. My singular expression, a smile.

Smiley Burk. The name given to me by Grandjesse, Daddy Ronnie's father. Always a smile for everyone, he said.

And the sweet one, everybody said. Not that Tommy wasn't sweet too; he just never seemed to care about coming across that way. Everyone loved him regardless. He wasn't mean, they realized—he just wanted something, all the time. Even if it meant picking fights with me.

"He was all over you," my relatives tell me. "Just hanging on you, all the time. I mean *all* the time."

But even then, I was Smiley Burk. Always a smile. Until, like my brother, I wanted something. The problem was, no one ever knew what I wanted. (How could they, when I didn't?) I would smile along happily through the day, and from one day to the next. Then, out of the blue, something would snap.

One day Grandaddy and Nanny saw it coming. But, apparently, there was nothing they could do to stop it. They were about to drive us somewhere and had placed me in the back-seat of their Volkswagen. When they returned with Tommy, I'd kicked a hole through the back of the passenger seat.

Smiley Burk.

"Nobody knows to this day what possessed you to do that, Scotty," Granddaddy chuckles.

An odd mixture of things, perhaps. Like those days when heavy raindrops fall, even though the sun is still shining.

2

My mother has said on rare occasions that she had only two blind dates in her life and she married both of them.

When Daddy Robert became our father, we began to learn what fathers do. He dressed smartly and neatly, and he was conscientious about our appearance. On Sunday mornings, he tried not to puff smoke in our faces as he raked Momma's steel comb across our tender heads. I stood as still as possible, in my khaki pants, white shirt, bow tie, and the loafers Daddy Robert had shined. He topped everything off by opening a bottle of cologne and peppering my face with his palm, saying, "Here, let's put some smell-good on you." When he'd finished, and I walked stiffly out of the bathroom, he whistled the Texaco tune behind me, "You can trust your car to the man who wears the star—," and Momma had to stifle her laughter.

Then he drove Tommy and me to Sunday school, handed us each a nickel or a dime for the collection plate, and dropped us off.

We placed our coins in the round, wooden plate that got passed around the table in class. But one day, as we were walking into the big church building, Tommy stopped me.

"Don't give them your nickel," he said knowingly. "Don't put it in the plate anymore. Just keep it."

"Why?"

"All they do is buy chairs with it."

I looked down at the tarnished coin in my palm. They used this to buy chairs? I thought this money went to God. That, somehow, it got all the way to heaven. That's where everything good was. How could they taint this God-money by using it here—*on chairs?*

I had a hard time imagining God when we were at church. He was everywhere, our teachers said, yet he was invisible.

But I had actually seen a picture of God. It was in a book at the doctor's office. God was a little boy, like my brother and me—with brown, curly hair, and a little round purple hat that sat on the back of his head. He was with his father, in a work-shop. After that, I supposed, he grew up to be God.

Yet that's how I continued to imagine him—in his purple hat, up on a cloud somewhere that was just big enough for him to play on. And every once in a while, God crawled over to the edge of the cloud—being very careful, so he wouldn't fall off— and he looked down at us all, and loved us.

In her first year of teaching, during the early sixties, my mother drove to a high school in a small town about ten miles away, called Midlothian. She was a fair but demanding teacher, and most of her students were bright and motivated. One student, however, always sat at the back of the class, slumped in his seat. His hair was dirty and his shirts were wrinkled. My mother never saw him talking to any other students. And he never volunteered anything in class. He always passed his tests, though, so she knew he was smarter than he let on.

She stopped him one day and confronted him about not turning in homework. I know you're bright, she told him. Why don't you do your assignments?

He shrugged impatiently.

She threatened to fail him if he didn't start doing his work. He wouldn't be able to graduate in May.

He said nothing. He wouldn't even look at her.

Undeterred, she told him she'd have to see his parents. She asked him for directions to his house, so she could drive out to talk to them the next afternoon.

He lived somewhere in the country. The directions led down a rural road, to a dirt drive she had to be careful not to miss. As she turned into the drive, she saw that it led to a small trailer home.

When she knocked, the student's mother opened the door. The woman's hair was mussed. She wore a thin house dress. Her face was lifeless.

"Come in," she said. The words were hateful.

My mother stepped inside. A pile of clothes sat in the middle of the room, three feet high. She looked down the short hallway to her student's room. He stood in the doorway, staring at her blankly. His room was barely larger than a library cubicle. Behind him stood an ironing board and another pile of clothes.

My mother cried the ten miles home. Something in her broke for him. He'd had everything taken away from him, before his life could even begin.

The next day, she asked the student if he would like to join the debate team. He raised his eyes in shock. He shrugged.

She made him join.

She challenged him, goaded him, cajoled him—continually tapping into something she knew was buried. And he responded. He became Midlothian's best debater. He won most contests against other schools, even the larger schools from Dallas. That spring, when the elimination tournaments began, he won at district and advanced to regional. He barely missed going to state.

And he changed. Day after day, she saw him getting stronger, more confident, trusting who he was and what he could do. At the end of the year, he was awarded a full scholarship to a large college.

He stood proudly at graduation. But afterward, he fell on my mother's shoulder, sobbing like a baby, and couldn't stop.

"Mrs. Sawyer—," he kept saying, then halting. "Mrs. Sawyer—"

He couldn't bring himself to say anything beyond her name.

She'd given him something, he thought—something that nobody could ever take away.

Daddy Robert hand-washed our station wagon in the driveway every Saturday. He took a plastic mop bucket, a sponge, and some rags, and wiped down the car, from the luggage rack to the hubcaps. He was thorough with every part, every angle and crevice. When he'd finished, it had a pure shine.

As he crouched down to clean the car's lower parts, his broad back spread wide. It curved both down and across, from shoulder to shoulder and neck to waist. When he worked on the hubcaps, the sinews in his arms bulged. Sometimes when he was crouching down, the top band of his underwear appeared just above the waist of his pants.

Occasionally, when my friend Laurie Green came into our yard to play, I tried to mimic my father's manly strength. I pretended to inspect some lower part of a fender, crouching down and arching my back in an effort to broaden it, or trying to flex my triceps. I also pulled down slightly on my pants to make sure the top of my underwear showed.

I'd seen most of the other fathers in the neighborhood, and none of them was like Daddy Robert. They either had stomachs hanging over their belts or crinkled pants or sheepish expressions or some other unforgivable deficiency. Even when Daddy Robert was in the front yard in his T-shirt—mowing grass or raking leaves or carrying garbage cans to the curb—he didn't look embarrassing. He might act embarrassed if someone he knew drove by and waved, but I knew deep down he wasn't.

Even our friends recognized Daddy Robert's whistle, from throughout the neighborhood. It didn't matter where we were when we heard it. We could have been wrestling in Bubba Meador's backyard or dog-piling on Benny McCuistion at our sandlot, The Circle. Or, Tommy might have been pulling a bigger kid off me, getting bloodied himself to keep me from being beaten. Whatever the case, when Daddy Robert's whistle came, we dropped everything and went. Or else.

The sound of his voice had the same startling effect. Once I climbed to the top of the thin chinaberry tree in our backyard, a height of some twenty feet. When Daddy Robert saw me through the kitchen window, he opened the back door and shouted, "Scotty! Get dow—"

He didn't get to finish. He'd so startled me, I lost my grip on the trunk. I fell backward, hurtling to earth—*bing! bing! bing!*—hitting every branch on the way down. Finally, my legs hooked over a sturdy lower limb, catching me. I was left swinging upside down, like a Christmas tree ornament.

But he surprised us. There was the time I had to perform in a kids' choir for a pageant, and Jumbo Stevenson cowed me into not singing. Jumbo, aptly named, stood grinning throughout the program, as I did beside him, never uttering a word. Afterward, my mother let me have it, as I'd expected.

"You didn't sing one word," she chided. "It was embarrassing."

I scuffed my shoes against the floorboard in the back seat.

"I couldn't *believe* it," Daddy Robert snorted from the driver's seat.

I looked up, surprised. He was glaring at me through the rearview mirror.

Daddy Robert—taking up for singing*? Mr. Kool, chastising me for refusing to do something sissy?*

My face grew red-hot with shame.

A former student of Momma's called to say he wanted to come visit her. He said he'd made something of himself, and he wanted her to see it. His name was Jimmy, and when he arrived we noticed he talked funny. Our parents were careful to talk slowly with him, as Jimmy ate dinner with us in our kitchen. He worked in a grocery store, he said, and great things were happening for him. With every tale he told about his work, he grew more excited.

At one point, Jimmy announced he'd like to race our father for fifty yards. Daddy Robert grinned and declined, but Jimmy wouldn't be refused. Momma looked doubtful. But Tommy and I begged our father to do it. We'd heard hints about his athleticism, but we'd never seen him in action.

Jimmy wouldn't relent. He walked outside and audibly stepped off fifty yards in the street, from our house to the Greens' down the block. Then he marched into the Greens' yard and took off his shoes, to run barefoot. Eventually, Daddy Robert followed him and took off his shoes too.

Momma sat with us in our front yard, marking the finish line. "On your mark," she said, "get set, go!"

They took off together. Jimmy started with long, loping strides. But Daddy Robert exploded into motion. I'd never seen anyone's legs move that fast. It was almost comical, like a cartoon character's.

As they got closer, our father no longer looked funny—he looked powerful. His head was lowered, his body leaning forward, his gaze straight ahead. He moved like a machine, all parts synchronized. No wavering, not even an inch.

"Go, Jimmy—beat him, beat him!" Momma yelled.

We stared at our mother. What was she saying? How could she yell against Daddy Robert?

"Go, Daddy!" we answered.

They passed the Johnsons' house. Next was Mrs. Forbes', then ours—the finish line.

Just before they got to our yard, Daddy Robert slowed down. He turned his head to watch Jimmy running slightly behind him. To our amazement, our father straightened up, relaxed his body, and slowed even more.

Jimmy never saw him. He was running straight toward us, his eyes wide, nostrils flaring. Daddy Robert finished a step behind him.

We couldn't believe our eyes.

"Woo woo, Jimmy," Momma said, clapping.

We ran up to our father. Tommy was crestfallen. "Daddy Robert," he said, "why'd you let him beat you?"

Our father shook his head, his face flushed. He turned to Momma and grinned. She was smiling at him, but kept praising Jimmy.

3

When our baby brother arrived, something told Tommy and me that all bets were off.

Buzzy. *Robert Meade Sawyer.*

This brother didn't look like either one of us. He had round features, like Daddy Robert's—round eyes, round nostrils, a turned-up nose. In fact, the only thing about our baby brother that didn't look like our father was his hair, which was red. Then Momma showed us a picture of Daddy Robert when he was a boy. There it was—red hair, discernible even in black and white. Our father was standing by the side of the house where he grew up—Poppy and Ween's house, across town from ours. And he looked just like Buzzy.

There were other differences. While Tommy and I freckled in the sun, our baby brother blistered. During the summers that followed, Buzzy had to wear a cowboy hat that turned down his ears, to keep his head from getting too sunburned. He also had boots to go with the hat—black, pointed boots. Boots we learned to hate because we ended up on their receiving end. Apart from Daddy Robert's wrath, those boots were Buzzy's only weapons against our agitation and torments.

Yet, when Buzzy first arrived—jumping out of our mother's stomach, as we understood it—Tommy treated him like a Christmas present. He wanted to hold him all the time, rock him, baby-sit him. I didn't know what to make of this sudden, drooling affection. Tommy acted as if he couldn't stand me most of the time. Now here he was, goo-gooing over somebody whose benefits had yet to be proven. Sooner or later, I figured, the other shoe was bound to drop.

I went back to our baby albums to verify the facts. Sure enough, there was a picture of Tommy in diapers, crying and grabbing onto the side of a bassinet. I asked Momma about this.

"He was trying to turn it over," she pointed out.

Why?

"He was mad. He didn't want you to be the baby," she said. "He gave you a black eye when you were two weeks old, Scotty. He threw a steel top into the bassinet and hit you with it."

Why'd he do that?

"He was jealous."

What does that mean?

"He didn't get to be the baby for very long," she said. "When you were born, Tommy still wanted to be the baby."

I had no idea what she was saying. Why would my older brother want to be a baby? Wasn't that the degrading name he always called me?

For the most part, we accepted Daddy Robert's punishments, knowing we deserved most of them. Yes, we were guilty—of tormenting our little brother and making him scream, alarming the whole neighborhood. Guilty of emptying the Flintstones Vitamins bottle and eating all the sweet pills at once. Guilty of leaving the outside faucet running all afternoon, turning the yard into a swamp we could stomp around in. Guilty of taking Momma's sewing scissors and cutting out pictures of women's naked behinds from a magazine we found in some bushes.

We dreaded the punishments we knew we were going to get. Yet this is exactly what puzzled me about Tommy's behavior. At times my big brother did things that were sure to provoke our parents' wrath. Even as I warned him of the hellish flames he was certain to feel, he plunged headlong into transgression, as if he were actually *seeking out* punishment.

Tommy didn't just cry when he was spanked. He *roared*, like a wounded animal. It embarrassed me. Buzzy and I might be sitting on the floor of his bedroom, playing some game, when we saw Daddy Robert pass by the door with a belt in his hand. Behind him was our big brother, his head lowered. They were headed toward the bathroom. Moments later, we heard the first crack of leather. It startled us, causing us to jump. Yet, when our fallen brother let out his hideous howl, we cupped our mouths to stifle laughter.

Nothing slowed Tommy down, though. When Buzzy got a baseball for his birthday, it turned up missing within days. This kind of thing turned my stomach into knots. We looked everywhere for it—under Buzzy's bed, under our bed, behind the living room couch. Are you sure it's not in your toy box? In your closet? Did you leave it outside? No, it's not anywhere.

Finally, Daddy Robert offered a reward to anyone who could find it.

Within minutes, Tommy appeared, palming the elusive ball. "Hey, look," he said.

"Yeah," Daddy Robert said, with a little laugh. It wasn't a real laugh.

I wasn't around when the ball was recovered. I asked Momma if Tommy got the reward for finding it.

"Uh huh," she said. "Daddy Robert gave him a knot on his head."

All three of us marked off the boundaries in our front yard for football. Buzzy and I were more meticulous about it. Sometimes we even hauled sand from our backyard sandbox to make hash marks. Tommy just wanted to get on with the game.

Buzzy had a football helmet that Daddy Robert painted whenever our little brother wanted to play for a different NFL team. One week it was the Eagles, the next week the Vikings, the next the Chiefs. Each week, the helmet got chipped whiter and whiter from our violent hits on our little brother. At times, I let myself go and hit Buzzy harder than I knew I should. I knew that if we got into trouble, I could probably hide behind Tommy's meanness. It was reliably worse.

I sensed whenever Tommy wasn't just playing a game with us. This day was one of those times. We played the usual way—

with two men on one side, kicking off to the third. When the third man caught the ball, he had to run through the other two, trying to get past them to score.

On the day I'm talking about, Tommy held nothing back. I could usually take my big brother's hits, because I was close enough in size to him. But Tommy didn't seem to care that Buzzy—as tough as he was—couldn't possibly absorb his hardest hits.

Buzzy had learned to run toward my side, to be tackled by me. But it didn't matter that day—Tommy got to him first every time. And he hit hard, headfirst.

Buzzy's outrage was loud each time.

"Quit it!"

"Shut up, baby."

"I'm not a baby. You're a *big* baby."

"*Little* baby."

Tommy was aware of what he was doing. What I couldn't understand was what possible reward there might be in it for him. Still, I said nothing. I knew Buzzy eventually would quit on his own, anyway. Yet it was so much worse today, I almost felt sick.

Buzzy ended up limping inside, crying.

"Go on, crybaby," Tommy said.

I was mad at my big brother. Did he actually think this made him tougher? Yet I felt sorry for him too. He had no idea how he looked doing this. It made me ashamed.

When Daddy Robert and Momma came home, they found Buzzy curled up on the couch. We knew that within minutes, one of our parents would come flying out of the house at us— hopefully Momma. But they didn't. Instead, the door opened slowly and Daddy Robert walked out carrying Buzzy. He put him in the station wagon, got in himself, and drove off.

We were afraid to ask Momma what happened. We were told later. The doctor had to take a needle and drain water out of Buzzy's knee.

We rarely heard the words that passed between our parents. Just the high pitch of Momma's shouts or Daddy Robert's sudden roars. Or a door slamming. Or, sometimes, an object hitting the floor.

It never occurred to us that we could lose one of them. We never let it cross our minds. Instead, we learned to laugh, the way we laughed at Tommy's spankings. We learned to turn down the sound, as I did at night when I heard Buzzy's muffled cries, coming from his room down the hall—hit by Tommy again. Or as I heard Tommy on the top bunk above me, whimpering—spanked again, because he'd been warned again. Again, again.

Why does he do it? I thought. He knows it's going to get him in trouble. He knows it every time. But he just keeps on. And why can't Buzzy just shut up and take it, to keep *them* from getting mad? Why?

My mother tells me she went to a minister in town back then. She wanted counsel about her marriage.

The minister's office was dark. As she spoke, she noted that his eyes darted around. He let her talk for a long time before he interjected:

—Have you ever thought about an affair?

She got up and left. Drove home trembling. She would never go back to him, or anyone like him.

If you're a perpetual pants-wetter, no day is a great day. When you come home from school with a foot-long, oval-shaped spot spilling down one pants leg, that's a bad day. When you come home with a small, circular, two- or three-inch spot—that's a good day. There are no great days.

This malady plagued me throughout first grade. I didn't have a dry day—not one. On the good days, I could successfully cover up to Momma when she picked us up after school.

"Scotty, did you wet your pants?"

"No," I lied.

I tried my best to stop. But it plagued me into second grade too. That year, it was only intermittent. Just two bad days the whole year.

In third grade, when I thought it was behind me, I was taken by surprise. Big, dripping pool around my desk. Fortunately, it happened just before recess. Mrs. Schick calmly asked me to stay behind as she filed everyone else out of the classroom. She summoned the janitor to clean up the mess and asked me if I wanted to go home to change. I was only too happy to go. I'd been walking to school by this time, and our house was only a few blocks away.

I dashed home, dripping wet. I looked through the closet to find my favorite shirt—the blue-and-purple plaid one. Then I pawed through our dresser drawer to find my favorite pants, the orange-and-white striped pair. I traded my brown leather loafers for my favorite shoes—the black-cloth track sneakers with malt-colored soles that curled upward at the toes.

I puffed back into class, just as my classmates were filing in. When Mrs. Schick saw me, she covered her mouth.

I told myself I didn't really *want* to avoid playing with Tommy. I liked being outside as much as he did. But he *always* wanted to play outdoors—usually football, even in summer. So I had to create believable reasons for not going outside with him. If he wanted to play after lunch, for example, I told him my food hadn't had time to digest. He rolled his eyes at this. What I really wanted was time to myself, so I could draw. A stack of paper and a pen—this, to me, was the best of all possible worlds. Making up my own comic strips. Dramatizing football games. Constructing forts—large, elaborate structures, manned by a rag-tag platoon of embattled soldiers, surrounded by enemies on every side.

When Tommy realized I was ensconced, occupying some shadowy interior, he gave up and went outside by himself. But not before he'd implanted an agitating thought in my head. This came just as he was exiting, a moment carefully timed for dramatic effect.

"Some people like to sit around and *draw* things," he said, careful not to name names. "Other people go out and *do* them."

A good number of my drawings involved someone dying in some dramatic form. If a character was evil, he might meet his end the DC Horror Comics way—say, going over a cliff, yelling, "Aaiiieee!" Or, if he were a Nazi soldier, I portrayed him in the throes of death—body crumpled, arms askew, eyes bulging as bullets sprayed through his torso.

If a character was heroic, however, he faced his demise nobly. I learned all the great ways to die well from The Dialing for Dollars Movie. If the feature was a western, the hero's sidekick might be mortally wounded. Say, a wooden plank had gone through his stomach after a bridge exploded—which actually happened to John Wayne's brother in *The Sons of Katie Elder.* But the sidekick would still be alive, with just enough breath to thank the hero for letting him come along for the ride. Then he would cough a few times, arch his back, roll his head to one side, and expire.

If you were watching a movie about a group of people on a life raft—for instance, *Sea Wife,* with Joan Collins and a half-dozen men, all trying to survive—you knew that by the end only one man would live to be the sea husband. And you could tell from the beginning who this guy was going to be—not the guy with a foreign accent, not the naïve young guy, not the greedy conniver. It would be the handsome guy who always knew the right thing to do.

When people weren't dying all over the place, The Dialing for Dollars Movies amounted to little more than grown-ups walking in and out of rooms wearing wool suits and skirts and lighting up cigarettes. I came to know all the great actors, though, because they turned up again and again. There was James

Arness—Marshall Dillon from "Gunsmoke"—taking on the giant ants in *Them*. And there was Forrest Tucker, apparently on sabbatical from "F Troop," fighting off *The Crawling Eye*. For my money, Warner Oland topped Sidney Toler as Charlie Chan. I shivered with awe as he whipped out a picture to reveal the killer, declaring, "The camera does not lie." He was right—a camera *doesn't* lie. The wisdom of the man!

Momma knew how I was spending my mornings and afternoons. Occasionally, she recommended a movie she'd noticed in the *TV Guide*. One day she told me I should watch one in particular, which I did. The only action that took place was at the beginning. In the opening scene, a little boy got hit by a truck and went deaf. The rest of the movie was about how the boy's mother, a widow, tried to cope with life and get him some kind of medical help. In the end, a nice trucker came along and married her, and adopted the boy.

The movie was something of a letdown. Most of it was beyond me—that is, except the *feelings* involved. I instinctively knew this was a movie my mother would cry over. And, I told myself, watching it had helped me enter a bit further into the mysterious, adult world she and Daddy Robert inhabited.

When Momma came home from teaching school that afternoon, I replayed the entire movie for her, in three or four sentences. I made sure I used all the sentiment I knew would affect her. Sure enough, her face took on a familiar longing that told me she wasn't going to cry but probably wanted to. It was a look, I thought, not unlike Lon Chaney's, when he heard the gypsy's violin and knew he was about to turn into the Wolfman and start turning tables over.

Then there was the movie star who looked most like Daddy Ronnie—James Garner. He had the same dark, wiry hair, the same dark eyes, the same dimple in his chin. And he looked pretty tall.

But James Garner acted too funny. He wasn't serious enough. In that way, he was nothing like Daddy Ronnie, I thought. If only James Garner knew this, the other people in the movie might like him better.

In the movie, he'd just gotten married to a dark-haired lady. But the problem was, he had another wife he thought was dead—a blonde—and now she'd come back and wanted to be his wife again. The blonde was mad at him now, because he'd gotten married while she was gone.

James Garner kept shushing the blonde and telling her to stay in the background. She had to give him time, he said, so he could tell his dark-haired wife about her. Sooner or later, though, you knew this blonde wife was going to come forward, and the dark-haired lady would find out about her. What would happen then? I thought. Which one really deserved to be his wife?

two

Places

4

Dear Everybody,
I hope Scotty has good grades. I hope I have good grades, too. And
Scotty, you are the best drawer I have ever seen. I hope Daddy Robert
gets paid Friday. And I hope Buzzy gets well soon.
With Love, Tommy

SEEING THOSE WORDS FROM MY BROTHER—"WITH LOVE"—
gave me a strange feeling. It made him seem even farther away
from us.

Tommy was the first to visit Brady. That was where Grandjesse and Tody lived—Daddy Ronnie's parents. (You pronounce
my grandmother's name "Toddy.") Their farm was hours away,
near the geographical center of Texas.

Tommy wrote letters to us every few days, mesmerizing us
with all the things he was getting to do—riding a tractor with
Grandjesse, feeding sheep, gathering eggs with Tody, seeing
jackrabbits, armadillos, scorpions, tarantulas, even rattlesnakes.
He came home wearing a T-shirt that read "Brady—The Heart
of Texas."

This summer, I was going with him. We would meet Grandjesse and Tody at the courthouse square in Cleburne, just as
we'd done the year before when Tommy went to the farm. I'd
remembered our grandparents driving up to our station wagon
in their old, roundish car. They emerged from it as if from
another era. Grandjesse wore a straw cowboy hat, and he stood
straight and tall. Tody wore a print dress and spectacles, her
gray hair curling softly over a round, sweetly smiling face.
Grandjesse's hawkish features broke into a grin as he shook
hands with Daddy Robert and saw us holding Momma's hands.

Once we were in the car with our grandparents, making the
long drive to Brady, the scenery began to change. The green
cotton fields Tommy and I were used to seeing became a yellow, sandy desert. Our towering, shady oak trees turned into
wind-bent mesquites. Suddenly, we could see farther. In the distance, scrubby hillsides sloped upward into flat-topped mesas.
It was magical, like watching a cowboy movie.

I gazed at the back of Grandjesse's neck as he drove. His
skin was lined with long crisscrosses, like a stretched-out
checkerboard. And it was dark orange, with crinkly white hairs
springing out of it. His neck looked like nobody's I'd ever seen.
I wondered how it got that way. I thought it must be the mark
of a wise, old man.

We were still an hour away from Brady when Grandjesse turned
off the highway onto a country road, just past a tiny town called
Blanket. It was a gravel road, leading toward a low ridge on the
eastern horizon. Halfway in between sat a wood-shingle house.
It was where Aunt Louisey and Uncle Pinky lived.

Aunt Louise was Daddy Ronnie's sister. At home, we had
faded-color pictures of her and Uncle Pinky. They were holding us as babies, trying to get us to smile. Aunt Louise had a
kind face, like Tody's. Now, as we saw her waiting for us in the
driveway, I noticed her hair had a touch of gray.

"Hello, sweet boys," she said. She gathered Tommy and me into a hug.

Sweet boys? Our aunt obviously didn't know us—at least not about our fights. As she looked into our faces, though, and smiled, her eyes crinkled at the corners—and I began to feel sweet.

Tommy ran to greet our cousin, Charles. He was the oldest—a hero, in our minds. We'd seen a picture of him in his football uniform for Blanket High School. And his three younger sisters—Martha, Colleen, and Laura—all were pretty, we thought. Later, Tommy and I would secretly argue over whose girlfriend Laura would be when we grew up.

After we ate lunch—sandwiches, with fresh sliced tomatoes from the garden—we gathered in the hallway, around an upright piano. Martha, the oldest, started pounding away. Laura stood next to her and began belting out "The Harper Valley PTA."

Tommy and I watched in awe. We'd never seen people do this kind of thing. It was like something you'd see on TV. Uncle Pinky must have noticed, and he joshed with us, poking fun. But Aunt Louise couldn't get over us. She looked at us as if we'd been away forever.

The sun seemed hotter on Grandjesse and Tody's farm. The sky was wide open, with barely a cloud, and even those clouds seemed higher and slower moving than the ones at home. We could see farther there than anywhere we'd ever been. Grandjesse's wheat fields stretched to the horizon. At a certain time of day, when the sun was high, we couldn't even see that far, unless we squinted our eyes. Everything looked blinding white. At times we even saw mirages along the dirt road leading to the pasture.

"That's the heat coming up from the ground," Grandjesse explained.

"It's not really water?" I asked.

"No," he grinned. "It's just the heat. It makes your eyes play tricks on you."

One morning we heard Grandjesse fire his shotgun. We ran out of the house and saw him standing by the barn. He was lifting a dead rattlesnake with the barrel of the gun.

"You blew his head off," Tommy said.

"Yep," Grandjesse said.

We followed him as he carried the snake toward a barbed-wire fence across the drive from their house. He slid the snake off the barrel and hung it over the fence, its white, lined belly facing upward.

"Why'd you hang that rattler there?" Tommy asked.

"Oh," Grandjesse began tentatively, "it's supposed to bring us rain." He grinned. We knew he didn't believe it.

Our grandfather moved slowly, but he always walked erect, his face aimed straight ahead. If he was walking toward the barn or the toolshed, and we called to him from behind, he turned his whole body around. He seemed older than our other grandparents—older than Tody too. But even after an entire day in the fields, he stood as arrow-straight as when he'd left. The band around his straw cowboy hat usually had a ring of sweat, and the top of his shirt was soaked. His face was red, and when he came inside and took off his hat, his thin gray hair lay plastered to his head.

As he sat down at the dinner table, he rested his palms on his thighs. He smiled at us and asked what we'd been doing.

"We hammered out pennies on the anvil," Tommy said. Or, we'd nailed two small pieces of wood together to make play pistols. Tommy carved his initials in everything he made: "TB."

Grandjesse sat as straight at the table as he walked. He didn't bend his head down to drink from his glass; he raised the glass to his mouth. That is, unless he was drinking coffee—then he sipped it out of the saucer. At breakfast, I noticed he used a knife as well as a fork to cut his eggs, which Tody cooked for him "over easy"—pink on top.

His eyes were set deep in their sockets. And when he laughed at something—always a low, quiet chuckle—his eyes brightened.

Sunday, July 27, 1969

Dear Everybody,

Scotty and I are having a ball. Last night we saw a skunk. Grandjesse shot at it and hit it, but it didn't die.

While we were up here we found a new place to play cowboys.

We went to see the old maids. Did you know Mr. Burger died a few months ago? He was a nice man.

We aren't going to get to ride the tractor because its two front tires are flat.

We've been looking at an old picture book.

We saw a western diamondback rattlesnake. Grandjesse blew its head off with the 4-10. Tody made some banana pudding. Wow, is she filling us up.

Is the new puppy Clyde doing o.k. with Buzzy?

We've been hearing owls at night. Grandjesse shot a jackrabbit and I found a turkey feather and stuck it in my hat.

I sure miss all of you.

Love, Tommy

P.S. Tody bought us some comics, b-b's, and caps for our cap guns.

We never heard Grandjesse talk about Daddy Ronnie. Tody did that. Her words about him were simple and plain. She ended each short statement with a soft, nervous giggle. She and Grandjesse let us sleep in Daddy Ronnie's old room. Some of his things were on the dresser—his fraternity picture, pictures of him running over hurdles, his track medals. Each medal lay in a small, thin box—either blue, red, or white, according to how he placed in a race.

We didn't see any football pictures.

"Did Daddy Ronnie like football?" Tommy asked.

"Yes, he did," Tody said.

"Who did he play for?"

"He played for Brady High."

She pulled open a drawer and lifted out a scrapbook. She opened it to show us pictures of Daddy Ronnie playing football.

We were relieved. He *had* to like football.

But he looked different from our other father in a football uniform. He looked skinnier than Daddy Robert, I noticed. Skinnier, like I was compared to Tommy.

After supper, we watched "The Mickey Finn Show" with our grandparents, or maybe a movie. One evening we got to see the Beatles' black-and-white movie, *A Hard Day's Night.* Grandjesse sat in his chair in the corner of the living room, while Tody sat on the couch. Our grandfather's chair was soft and had his smell. Next to it, a Bible sat on a small reading table. On the nights we didn't watch TV, Grandjesse told us jokes and asked us for some. Sometimes he just sat quietly, while Tody did some kind of handiwork and we played a game on the floor.

One sleepy evening, I lay on the carpet beside Grandjesse's chair, my head cradled on my hands. I watched a tiny scorpion emerge from nowhere and slowly make its way toward me. I was too drowsy to move. Just as it got close, however, the big Bible dropped on it. Crushed the scorpion right before my eyes.

Once, Grandjesse wanted to play catch with me. I was afraid he might be too old—that I'd knock him over if I really zipped the ball to him. I wondered if he thought I was a sissy.

He walked to the whitewashed storage shed near the barn and pulled out two old, dried-out gloves. They were stiff, with the leather chipping off. We had to punch them a few times to soften them up.

He only had a softball, not a hardball.

"Was this Daddy Ronnie's softball?"

"Yes, it was."

I'd never imagined our father playing with this kind of glove or ball. In fact, I'd never imagined him playing baseball or softball at all. Just football and track.

Grandjesse threw the ball to me. When I caught it, I threw it back to him underhand.

He teased me. "Don't throw it underhand," he said. "That's the way girls throw."

I zipped the next one to him. I was careful to be accurate, though, so the ball wouldn't get past him.

He caught the throw easily and tossed the ball back to me slowly. His throw was accurate.

I threw harder the next time.

He smiled. "That's the way," he said.

We played catch that way for a long while.

Tody had brought in all of Daddy Ronnie's old comic books from the storage shed—Classics Illustrated, DC Horror Comics, paperback books of *Mad* magazine cartoons. That evening, Tommy and I sat on the front porch with Grandjesse, flipping through the comics. Our grandfather sat in his metal porch chair, listening to a baseball game on his transistor radio.

Behind us, on the back side of the house, the sun was descending over the wheat fields. It caused the sky in front of us to change slowly from orange, to pink, to purple, to bright blue.

Our grandfather sat silent and still, his hands resting on the chair's rails. The low voices from the radio hummed like a lullaby.

"Who's playing?" Tommy asked.

"It's the Houston Astros," Grandjesse said.

I gazed across the highway that stretched in front of our grandparents' house. I wondered how we could hear a game being played as far away as Houston. I thought we were too far out in the country to hear anything familiar.

I looked at Grandjesse. He just sat listening, his eyes gazing out across the highway too, into the clear evening blue.

5

Daddy Robert's father owned a farm too. Poppy's farm was just outside of Waxahachie. It was a cotton farm, a large one, with the land stretching out in a series of narrow, ridged rows. The neat rows were broken up only by an occasional patch of trees, or a tiny creek, or a livestock tank like the ones on Grandjesse's farm. If we were on Poppy's farm in the summer, when the cotton plants were green and full, the fields looked like a broad swatch of corduroy. If we were there during the fall—on the day that Daddy Robert went dove hunting—the ground was cold and flat. The dirt was dark gray, black when it was wet. After a rain, we could hardly walk through it.

Daddy Robert usually returned from his annual hunting day with a handful of doves. Momma cooked them once, frying them like chicken. That evening, Tommy bit into a piece of buckshot. He held up the jagged metal, grinning, as if it were a treasure.

One year, Daddy Robert decided to take Tommy and me along with him on his dove-hunting day. He let us bring an old BB gun, so we could shoot at tin cans. He held the gun in our arms, while we took aim and fired off rounds.

After we finished target practice, he decided to go shoot at some doves. He instructed us to stay in a specific spot, near a stock tank, so we'd be safe.

He'd been walking for ten minutes or so when he turned and saw us following him.

"I thought I told you to stay back there."

"We thought you were gonna leave us."

"Leave you? Why would I leave you?"

"We don't know."

Mom tells me she went to see a psychologist about us. About Tommy, in particular.

—Where on earth did you find a psychologist?

—I had to go to Dallas. I can barely remember it. I know it was expensive. I just didn't know what else to do.

The psychologist explained that Tommy simply wanted a father. Mom came home and told Dad about it. She said, You've got to be a daddy to him, Robert. You've got to do things with him. Just little things. Take him to the store with you. Let him ride around with you on your errands.

Daddy Robert made an agreement with Tommy. He needed help with the empty deposit bottles around the house, he said. He wanted Tommy to help gather them up, load them into the car, and help unload them at the grocery store. If Tommy did that, he could keep whatever deposit money they got in return.

Overnight, my big brother became king of something besides Buzzy and me. He reveled in the job. He also started helping Daddy Robert with other tasks around the house. He lobbied to help set up something our father had bought called a "Cowboy antenna." When our team, the Dallas Cowboys, played at home, the games were blacked out—meaning, you couldn't watch them if you lived within a certain radius of Dallas. To get around these blackouts, you had to buy a Cowboy antenna—an elaborate wire that picked up broadcasts from a Waco station and beamed them back to your set. Even though the picture was snowy, you still got to watch the games.

To set up the antenna, Daddy Robert stationed himself at the very top of the roof, where it sloped down on either side. He held the antenna in place, while Tommy sat nearby and carefully retrieved the tools I threw onto the roof from the front yard.

"Scotty," Tommy would yell down, "go get us a Phillips head screwdriver."

Daddy Robert kept his tools in a drawer in the kitchen. I would go inside, poke through the drawer and hopefully find the right tool. If I didn't, I panicked. In that case, I had to go back outside and ask what the tool looked like. Tommy would look down at me, shaking his head in disgust. Daddy Robert then shouted out a description of the tool, and I'd go back inside and scratch around in the drawer again. Finally, I would find it, sigh in relief, and dutifully deliver it.

This went on for most of the afternoon. We were nearing completion of the antenna setup when I was sent to the kitchen for one final tool, a crescent wrench. As I walked past the TV, its flickering image caught my eye. A monster movie was showing—Saturday's "Nightmare Theater" feature. It was the one where turtle-looking creatures with long necks and pin heads made radioactive sounds and were attacking England. Kirby Renfro had told me about this movie. Whenever somebody killed one of the turtle creatures, yellow stuff that looked like chicken noodle soup poured out of them. Peter Cushing was one of the scientists who was trying to kill them. He was wearing, oddly enough, a black turtleneck.

Now a group of scientists, similarly clad, were creeping through a marsh with Peter Cushing. They were carrying silver, ray-gun type weapons. You could hear radioactive sounds going off nearby, so you knew the turtle creatures were somewhere in the cattails. And you knew one of the guys in the group was going to get killed. I tried to determine which one it would be. If a woman was along, she would be safe—a woman in the group was usually the head scientist's girlfriend. But there was no woman here. Might there be among these men a scientist with thick glasses—one who handled his weapon awkwardly and looked as if he didn't know what he was doing? He would be the one to get it. Or, was there an innocuous-looking scientist in the group, some guy you hadn't noticed before? That's the guy who would get killed.

I realized this was only the middle of the movie. I could tell because the main stars weren't getting killed yet. Only at the end of the movie would the people you liked be getting picked off by the turtle creatures, one by one. And it would be happening in the middle of London, because the turtle creatures would have finally worked their way there, intent on the total annihilation of—

Ow—my head.

I turned and saw Tommy. He'd slapped me.

"Dummus," he said.

He went to the kitchen and rummaged through the tool drawer. A minute later, he emerged and planted himself between the TV and me. He held up the crescent wrench.

"What does this look like?" he accused.

It was something I'd heard Daddy Robert say.

Tommy shook his head. "You may have book sense, but you don't have any common sense." He stomped out self-righteously.

My homemade comic strips had begun to evolve into several series. My specialty was a military comedy I titled "The Adventures of Private Dunce." In it, a hapless enlisted man worked up scheme after self-serving scheme. He always ended up getting his just deserts, with something akin to a bang on the head.

About the same time, Tommy started writing a series of stories. He'd dabbled in writing before, his first stories about the misadventures of a goofy character named Pepecek. He'd based the character on a kid he'd seen in an episode of the Saturday morning "International Children's Film Festival." Tommy thought the name *Pepecek* itself was funny. And, like my Private Dunce, his Pepecek was constantly getting into trouble.

Now, however, Tommy's stories were markedly different. These were detective stories, in which he starred with his real-life friend, Johnny McAdams. As each story began, he and Johnny consulted their boss—just as Robert Wagner did at the beginning of each episode of "It Takes a Thief." At the end, they reported back to their boss, returning some stolen goods or turning in some cuffed culprit. Then they walked away coolly. The stories were light-years from the ne'er-do-well Pepecek.

6

I woke to yells somewhere in our house.

"Help! Help me!"

Then, Momma's voice. "Shh, Robert. Wake up."

The next morning I asked my mother what had happened.

"Your Daddy had measles when he was little," she said. "Back then, they thought the measles could make you go blind. The doctors made him lie in a dark room with the shades down."

That's why he screams now?

"Yes. He's having nightmares about it."

I thought of Daddy Robert's brawny back, his hands, his muscles. Our father was scared?

Occasionally, when we stumbled into the kitchen early enough on a weekday morning, we saw a paper plate on the table with writing on it. The writing was usually in some bright-colored ink, from a felt-tip pen. Its message was from Daddy Robert to Momma. At the bottom, just above his name, was a cryptic closing: "21".

We begged our parents to tell us the secret of this mysterious number. But neither of them would.

Just as mysterious to me was the first time Daddy Robert gave us each a box of candy for Valentine's Day. He left the boxes on the kitchen table, with homemade cards and notes to us inside.

His gesture embarrassed me. It was the way you'd show love for a girl, not a boy. I couldn't imagine my friends' fathers doing the same for them.

But my feeling quickly changed. What Daddy Robert did for us on Valentine's Day made me feel big. Because *he* had done it.

Buzzy's elementary school was near Poppy and Ween's house. He often stayed with them after school, until Momma came to pick him up.

One day Buzzy came to us grinning. "Guess what Ween told me about Daddy?" he whispered. "She said they built the front porch for Daddy to dance on." He giggled goofily.

Tommy and I looked at each other.

"I wonder if he and Momma danced out there," Tommy said. Buzzy looked puzzled.

"What were you thinking, idge?" Tommy said.

"I thought Ween meant *tap* dancing," Buzzy said. "You know—like, putting on shows for people."

We all howled at the idea. None of us could envision our father *tap dancing* for anybody.

All three of us began soaking Ween and Poppy for stories about Daddy Robert. Poppy gladly told and retold our father's high school football exploits. Ween delighted in disclosing more personal details.

"You never saw anyone wear such colorful clothes," she said. "He dressed like Jimmy Demaret, the golfer. And you never saw someone so shy. I'd drop Bobby off at the high school, and he'd walk straight into the building. All his friends would be waving, 'Hi, Bobby, Hi, Bobby.' He never even looked up. He just ducked his head and went straight inside."

We relished repeating these anecdotes to Daddy Robert. And we could predict his reaction to them. He winced, snorted, stamped his foot, shook his head in anguish. And we laughed. Our powerful father was rendered helpless by a great disparity—the chasm we saw existing between family myth and personal truth. As Daddy Robert's face turned redder and redder, we laughed all over again. His wrath was something funny now, because it was aimed at someone else.

We all were in grade school at the time—Tommy in sixth, I in fifth, Buzzy in first—when we learned that Princess, our border collie, was going to have puppies. Momma checked out a stack of books about dogs from the library so we could be prepared for the delivery when it came. My brothers and I sat in on some of the learning sessions our parents held in preparation for the births. A lot of this had to do with taking precautions, what to expect when the puppies came, how many would survive, and so forth.

But what stirred us most was the danger involved. We understood that some of the puppies would be born dead. And we learned that some who would appear to be dead would actually still be alive, and that Princess would ignore them. We had to be careful to look out for those puppies who would appear dead but might still be living.

Buzzy was up early that cold morning. He came in with the news: "Princess had her puppies."

We all ran out to the garage. We saw the mother lying wearily in the blanketed nest Momma had built for her. She was surrounded by tiny, crawling creatures, exploring their new world.

"Look," Tommy said. He pointed to a dead pup lying beside a garbage can. Its skull had caved in. We inspected it briefly before discovering another dead pup nearby. Both had been abandoned by Princess, who was concerned with feeding the live ones.

My brothers and I followed the tiny pups around on the garage floor as they slowly crawled about like slugs. Daddy Robert picked up each of the dead pups to examine them. He took a close look at the one whose head was intact.

"Is he alive, Robert?" Momma asked.

He and Momma disappeared into the house, while we picked up Princess's puppies, smelled them, stroked them. We were there for maybe half an hour before we got too cold and had to go inside to get our jackets. As we turned down the hall, we could see into our parents' bedroom.

Daddy Robert was sitting on the edge of the bed, hunched over. He had the dead puppy on his lap, pressing its stomach. The puppy's chest and belly moved up and down grotesquely, like a balloon inflating and deflating. Its tiny limbs flailed like a doll's each time Daddy Robert applied his thumb. The dog's mouth was open, its tongue hanging out. It looked dead.

It was too harsh for me to watch. I turned away. How could Daddy Robert do that? I thought. What if the puppy was alive? Our father was too strong to press on its stomach that hard. He could be hurting the dog. And, if it was still alive, he might even kill it.

We put on our jackets, and Tommy picked up an old blanket. We went back to the garage, where Tommy spread out the blanket next to Princess's nest. Then we rounded up all the pups and put them on it.

A while later, Momma came outside carrying one of the puppies. It was the one we'd thought was dead. Our mother was smiling. The pup looked up from her arms, sniffing around blindly.

"Daddy Robert brought him alive," Tommy said.

I'd thought our father might kill the pup without meaning to. But he hadn't. He'd brought it back to life. It was a miracle.

We called him King. We gave the other puppies unimaginative regal names too, in honor of the mother, Princess: Queen, Duke, Prince. But there was something that moved me about King's name. He'd been dead—I'd seen him with my own eyes, lying there lifeless. And then he was alive.

7

Once a year, we took a family vacation to Austin. It was where Daddy Robert had gone to college, at the University. In the afternoons, we swam in the pool at our motel, the Villa Capri. At night, we drove around the city, looking at things.

One night we passed a large hospital that took up a whole block. It had a huge lawn and was surrounded by a tall chain-link fence. We noticed barbed wire strung across the top of the fence.

"What's that place?" Tommy asked.

"It's the mental hospital, honey," Momma said. "Daddy Robert used to work there."

We gazed at the building somberly.

"Crazy people live there?" Tommy asked.

"Yep," Daddy Robert answered. He said this matter-of-factly.

We scanned the lawn for crazy people but saw none.

"Why do they have bob wire on top of the fence?" Buzzy asked.

"So the patients can't leap it," Daddy Robert said.

We laughed wildly at the idea of crazy guys trying to high-jump a ten-foot fence.

Next, we drove by Memorial Stadium, where the Longhorns played. The stadium was huge, with floodlights lighting it as if it were a monument.

"You went to games there, didn't you?" Tommy asked.

"Sure," Daddy Robert said.

The next afternoon, we drove back to the stadium. Adjacent to it was an open practice field made of Astroturf. Daddy Robert and Momma sat in the shade of some live oak trees, while we passed the football around on the turf. We imagined ourselves to be young Longhorns as we ran, threw, and tackled in the shadow of the stadium walls.

He hadn't come to Austin on a football scholarship, as the Dallas writers had predicted.

Bobby Sawyer—not *voted All-District,* one *scribe had harrumphed, because they didn't allow* sophomores *on the team.*

The next year, as a junior, he wrecked his knee. Then it was over.

It had rained the day before. The sun had dried out the ground, making it a concrete slab. The coaches ordered a few scrubs to get some hoes and chop it up, so the team could practice. When they handed him the ball on the first play, he planted and cut, to get past a linebacker. Everybody heard the pop, all the way across the field. Their heads turned just in time to see him go down.

The doctors didn't have scopes in those days. They cut you open, sliced around, and sewed you back up. He was lucky to come out walking straight.

He enrolled as a premed student and looked around for a night job at a hospital. This one had an opening.

Thursdays were insulin shock treatment days. The patients had to line up outside the door—all crew cuts, stubble, and wrinkled scrubs. If a cafeteria worker happened to walk by with an open barrel of sugar, the patients lunged for it. If there was any sugar in their system, they didn't have to get shocked.

He only had to see this once.

He brought Patricia down for a fraternity party on a riverboat. The Dekes had gotten kicked off campus for throwing beer cans from their homecoming float. He wasn't one of the wild ones, though—he just liked the other guys. On the bottom deck of the boat they were partying like animals. He took Patricia to the top, where they could slow dance by themselves. He was a gentleman, doing the little things that charmed her, such as sweetening her iced tea in restaurants.

He was home, in Waxahachie, the next summer. They were sitting in his car, in front of her house, when she asked him what he wanted to be.

"A minister," he said.

She laughed.

He went back to UT that fall. She went to North Texas State.
Word got back to him she was dating someone. A track guy.

A name came up during that Austin trip, one we'd never heard before.

Momma said it: "Suzy."

Daddy Robert was quiet. He just kept driving.

Momma stared at him. Then she punched him—hard—in the arm.

"Ow."

We half-flinched, half-laughed in the backseat. This had the smell of a good rumble.

"Who's Suzy?" I asked.

"His ol' *girl*friend," Momma said in mock disgust. "From college."

Daddy Robert shook his head. I saw him grinning in the rearview mirror.

"He *says* she looked like Kim Novak," Momma said. "Ween always told me she looked just like *me.*"

Daddy Robert jabbed back.

"What about *Christy*?" he said.

Momma tried to cover her smile. We'd seen pictures of her high school boyfriend from Louisiana. He wore glasses like Granddaddy's and huge, baggy swimming trunks. He also did embarrassing, girlish things for the camera. We couldn't picture our mother with this guy. Even Nanny had said, "Oh, all Christy ever did was toot that old horn." *He played a horn. And he had a girl's name!*

Their jabs went back and forth, along with their laughter, a brief skirmish.

I'd always been curious about what made our parents laugh. For Momma, it was usually Jerry Lewis or Peter Sellers doing what she called "silly business." Daddy Robert laughed at those guys too, but he was baffled by the disabling effect they had on our mother. Out of nowhere, Momma would be struck with an affliction they called "the dubs." First she fell silent, as if the wind had been knocked out of her. Her chin dropped to her chest and she sat still for a minute, her eyes closed, her mouth frozen in a laugh. Then her shoulders began heaving. Slowly, she tilted to one side, as if she'd lost the use of her limbs. Finally, she collapsed in a heap—on the bed, the couch, the floor. It didn't matter where she was at the time.

Tommy and I occasionally witnessed the onset of the dubs during Momma's play practices with her drama students. Some student would say something he didn't know was funny, and Momma was overcome. First, the room went silent. Then our mother's head started bobbing. Slowly, Momma sank down in her seat, until she was out of our view. At that point, we had to watch the students' eyes onstage to know when she'd hit the floor.

When Tommy was in sixth grade, Momma cast him in one of her high school productions, *Our Town*. He played a paperboy, and he came home from practices telling stories about Momma's students as if he were buddies with them. The night of their dress rehearsal, he ate supper with makeup on. "Graham Compton was walking around backstage in his underwear," Tommy marveled. "He was smoking a cigarette and yelling at everybody like they didn't know what they were doing."

I didn't see the play all the way through until opening night. It was only then, in the middle of the story, that I learned Tommy gets killed. He grows up and goes to war and then dies on the battlefield. This doesn't happen onstage; the narrator tells us about it. What a waste, I thought. I thought of all the ways I could have tutored Tommy in how to die nobly. But he would never get to do it. Still, it was just like a movie.

That fall, we all drove to Brady, to Grandjesse and Tody's farm. Grandjesse had suffered a heart attack. He was sitting in his chair when we saw him, smiling and talking to us as he always had. His neck looked a little thinner, and he spoke more softly than usual. Other than that, though, he seemed fine to us. Daddy Robert asked him questions about his operation. I thought we all might spend the night, but that afternoon we drove back home.

A month later, Aunt Louise called. Our grandfather had died.

On October 22, 1971, Tommy and I wore our favorite nice clothes to school. We were in eighth and seventh grades. The class I had just before lunch was Miss Kraft's earth science class. I sat next to my best friend, John Martin—Big John, my basketball partner. John was the one who, on the first day of school, had noticed I'd written my name differently on an assignment:

"Scotty Sawyer."

Not Scotty Burk, as I'd always been known.

"'Sawyer'?" he'd asked.

I'd nodded.

His eyes had searched mine for signs, trying to determine whether it was appropriate to ask anything more. Or, maybe he was trying to see if there was anything truly different about me because my name had changed.

It had never occurred to me that anyone *would* see me differently. I'd never given a second thought to my name being Burk and my parents' Sawyer. I didn't think my friends did, either. But Daddy Robert and Momma had. And on that day in October, dressed in our favorite nice clothes, Tommy and I were getting out of school early, just before lunchtime, to go to the courthouse. Daddy Robert was adopting us.

He hadn't prepped us much for the ceremony. I was surprised when the judge sounded serious about most of the things that came up. He asked us questions with a gravity that didn't mean much to us. Our father seemed calm, so we were calm too.

At the end, the judge told us, "Boys, you can change your last name from Burk to Sawyer. Or, you can keep Burk and just add Sawyer to the end."

We looked at our father. We didn't know how to answer.

He just patted our shoulders.

Afterward, he took us to Brookside Inn, the best restaurant in town, for a nice lunch.

"I want you to do something for me," he said.

Tommy and I were glad to oblige him.

"Don't tell Buzzy we did this. This is just for us."

three

Legs

8

July 14, 1971

Dear Tommy,

You're probably wondering, "Why the watch?"

I'm sure you know all about tradition. When Jewish boys reach the age of 13, there is the Bar Mitzvah. When other races of the world reach 13, there are various other types of ceremonies that celebrate the boy becoming a man. Well, in my family, or at least for me, it was receiving a wristwatch; this was my tradition. So, I'm giving you this watch that celebrates your becoming a man.

I know, after being with you while Mom was gone last summer, that there is no finer boy than you. You're a good child, and I love you very much. I want you to know that I always have faith in you, and believe that you will be a fine man.

On becoming a man, there are responsibilities that you will for the first time inherit. The ability to face disappointment, to feel compassion for those less fortunate than you, to help those weaker than you, to show kindness and understanding when it seems almost impossible. And, probably the most important of all, reliability.

So . . . I hope you like the watch, and congratulations on becoming a man on this your 13th birthday.
Love always,
Dad

IT WAS A KIND OF WATCH WE'D NEVER SEEN BEFORE. IT HAD A dark face, with three rings of numbers on it, and a plastic ring around the rim. The ring allowed you to time things. Dad said it was a skin-diver's watch. It was cool because it wasn't a toy— it was a man's gift.

I was already at home, after the first day of school, when Mom and Tommy came in. Tommy's hair was wet from showering after football practice. They were silent as they walked through the door. Tommy had a defeated look. Mom looked agitated. This wasn't about football.

"What happened," I said.

"His watch got stolen," Mom said. She walked briskly into the kitchen.

"Somebody broke into my locker," my brother said weakly. Mom wasn't mad at Tommy. She knew Dad would be.

He had just finished his last Little League season with me. We'd played on the same team, Flexsteel, for two years. The league rule was that brothers had to play on the same team.

Tommy batted in the spot behind me. He'd always swung awkwardly, bending his elbows and holding his arms close to his body. He didn't get extension, the way I'd learned to do. That summer, the pitches didn't look fast coming toward me anymore, as they had before. Now every throw came in slow motion, and I didn't have trouble making contact. I even grazed a few of Darrell Wilson's curveballs—the nastiest pitch from the league's most feared pitcher. Darrell was older, Tommy's age, and he'd thrown a one-hitter against us. Our lone hit was my drive to center.

If I was on base when Tommy came to the plate, he usually left me stranded. It happened again in our final game together. It was a late inning, and we were behind by a run. I'd doubled and stood on second, the potential tying run. As Tommy stepped into the batter's box, I took a cautious lead toward third. A screechy noise began building in the bleachers. The parents always let you know when you were in an important situation.

The count quickly went to two strikes, on successive pitches. I willed it not to happen, *not to happen.* Of course, it did.

I crouched off second, ready to sprint to third. The next few seconds expired in slow motion. The throw came in over the plate . . . Tommy waited till the last second before swinging . . . he swung tightly, as he always did—blindly, not watching the ball in . . . he missed it by a foot . . . a groan went up from the bleachers.

I knew Tommy hadn't wanted to be there. He only played because I played. Baseball had no payoff for him, no outlet—no contact, no *hitting.* Same in basketball. I loved the clean economy of the bank shot, the well-executed fast break, the calculated rhythm of the last two strides before laying the ball off the glass. Tommy always went up for a lay-up off the wrong foot.

He learned to deflect his deficiencies with humor. If we were playing in a pickup game with friends and he made a rare basket, he spiked the ball, football-style. Afterward, as we walked home, he reminded me of a Vince Lombardi maxim, with vindictive relish. "Basketball is a contact sport," he quoted. "Football is a *hitting* sport."

My big brother might have written me off for specializing in the softer sports. But he was still determined to make Buzzy tough. He no longer looked to our little brother to provide any real competition in football; Buzzy was still too young even for the peewee league. But Buzz did excel in the annual Punt, Pass & Kick competitions. Now Tommy enlisted him to build a goalpost together, so they could practice kicking. They took a few one-by-fours, nailed them together, and planted them at the far end of our front yard, just beyond the driveway. That way, they had the entire length of the yard to practice kicking balls.

Their only hazard was a thick, massive tree in our front yard. They learned to kick around it, as if it were a charging lineman. But they practiced so often, and so relentlessly, inevitably a ball was sent flying into the tree and got stuck. The tree had no lower limbs, so it was impossible to climb up to retrieve the balls. It just kept eating whatever my brothers kicked into it.

The summer before I entered seventh grade, my parents signed me up to go to an art camp in Kansas. They knew I loved to draw, and I'd won a few awards at the junior high art fair. They may have thought I showed some promise beyond the cursory assignments I did for my art class.

I was still drawing in my free time, mostly at school after I'd finished an assignment. I always used blank paper, and I always drew in ink—always. If I messed up at some point, I started over. So I was very careful to get things right. I had to take into account everything I was going to do before I actually did it.

Once I was involved in a drawing, I disappeared. I became completely absorbed—entering the world I created on paper, feeling the lines as I drew them, as if they were extensions of my own limbs. Long, angular lines that formed a language nobody else spoke—vertical and horizontal, one after another, filling the whole page, an entire interior world, from one border to the other. When I'd finished and looked up, I realized I'd lost track of everything else—of time, space, even my whereabouts. I was embarrassed if anyone had been watching.

I hadn't wanted to go to the art camp. And I couldn't have known how inexplicably scared I would be once I got there. For the first time, I was going solo into unfamiliar territory. The camp was in Lawrence, Kansas, at the university. My roommate was a tall, friendly high-schooler named Dave—kind, open, generous, always inviting me to have lunch with him and his girl-friend. But I declined each invitation. I ended up staying in my room most of the time.

The sessions were nothing like what I'd expected. We painted the inside of a cigar box black and drilled a pinhole in it, to make a homemade camera. We inched objects across a table, millimeter by millimeter, all week long, just to make a six-second film. I couldn't believe this was why I'd come. It didn't seem to have anything to do with art. Nothing I was doing gave me the satisfaction I got from drawing.

Every evening after supper, I went to my room and lay in bed. My insides were in knots all the time. Why did I feel this way? Why did I cry every night? I was about to enter eighth grade, for goodness' sake.

Evidently, Mom and Dad knew I'd get homesick right away. They had the foresight to make my brothers sit down and write to me on the day I left. Mom wrote at length about Tommy and his new friend, Darrell Wilson, the hellacious pitcher. Darrell was also the quarterback for Tommy's football team. This year, Tommy was determined to be a receiver instead of a lineman, so he'd paired up with Darrell to practice passing and catching. Now they did most other things together, Mom said. They swam, started a weight-lifting program, ran laps around the junior high track.

Mom encouraged me to get out and meet people, that maybe I'd get a scholarship to Kansas when I graduated. She tried to lighten things up at the end with a description of the ongoing fraternal conflicts: "Buzzy just did something to Tommy and Tommy yelled, 'Quit it!' and started beating him around all over my bed. I don't know why everyone has to come to my room to write their letters."

Dad's humor was intact: "Not much happening here. I had the squirts, Clyde chased some birds in the yard—you know, the usual stuff. . . . If you don't have anything to do Sunday, why don't you tour the campus and see where they play football?

Maybe they have a 'hall of fame' where they keep old jerseys (Gale Sayers, Wilt Chamberlain, etc.). Some colleges have great museums (you know how I like museums). Well, as I said, not much news. If you have time, why don't you write Tody? She would be so happy to hear from you."

Tommy wrote a short note, trying to shore me up. He threatened to beat up my roommate, whomever he might be, if he gave me any trouble. Buzzy got straight to the point: "How are you? Who is your roommate? Are you having fun? We lost 8 to 4. Have fun."

On Sunday, I dutifully went to the places on campus where they hung the jerseys. I wanted to be able to tell them I'd seen them.

9

Not long after I got home, we moved into a different house. It was on East University, down the street from the Assemblies of God college. At the other end of the street was the Wilsons' house, where Darrell lived. Now he and Tommy were within a block of each other.

I'd never been away from Tommy for that long, I realized. Things had changed while I was gone. My brother had hair under his arms now, and even a few hairs on his chest. He and Darrell were working out every day at the junior high football field. They came home exhausted, grass blades plastered to their calves. Tommy had been running pass patterns, Darrell pinpointing his throws to him. Darrell always had an air of cool about him, so that he never looked exhausted, even if he was red-faced and panting. This was something else that had changed in my brother, I noticed. Before, whenever he'd done something exhausting, he always looked as if he were about to collapse. Now he wore the same air of cool as Darrell.

When the junior high gym wasn't open, they lifted weights in our garage. Dad had bought Tommy some free weights the year before—the round kind, made of concrete encased in plastic. Sometimes Tommy and Darrell were lifting when I went outside to shoot baskets. Their talk was usually about girls, but it was always indirect. Neither of them ever said he *liked* a girl. Instead, they cracked jokes about one's physical attributes. Or they made cryptic references to having spoken with one. Maybe they'd gotten a ride home with an older girl, or they'd seen one riding a bike through the neighborhood. They acted as if they couldn't stand some of them, but their reasons were never clear to me.

At night, Tommy sneaked out with Darrell to meet up with other guys. He said they were going to "wrap" houses—throwing toilet paper rolls over them and through the trees. It was always a girl's house, some girl that one of them liked.

I didn't understand. Why would you wrap some girl's house if you liked her? She'd have to spend the whole next morning cleaning up what you did. Wouldn't that make her mad?

One afternoon, I found a notebook in the nightstand drawer between our twin beds. It was full of poetry—Tommy's poetry. He was writing about a girl—her eyes, her hair, her mouth. The effect she had on him.

He broke into the offensive lineup that year—tight end. He wasn't that fast, so he wasn't the coaches' first choice as a receiver. But Darrell knew him—knew where he'd cut, where he'd be open, and that if he got the ball to Tommy, he'd catch it. It didn't happen often, but when it did, it was effective.

In their first game, Darrell called a look-in lateral—a pass to the tight end, who caught the ball and pitched it backward to a flanker streaking by. Tommy ran eight yards and turned. Darrell's pass was high, and Tommy had to leap for it. Somehow, my brother knew the defender was right behind him—so, as soon as he caught the ball, he pitched it back while still in midair. Sam Hargers took it for a long gain—a crowd pleaser. Suddenly, the screeching from the bleachers sounded good.

One evening, a half dozen of Tommy's teammates had amassed in our back bedroom. They decided to play "goal line" on their knees—but they weren't on their knees for long. Soon they were diving over a pile of bodies, trying to cross an invisible goal line.

When Mom heard the slamming of bodies and crashing of furniture, she stormed into the room.

"Tommy," she barked, "you're going to end up with a broken beak, like Daddy Ronnie."

"Beak," the guys crowed. "Beak!"

They all had nicknames: Dragon, Scum, Sax, Potty (short for Potty-AH-tah), Chalky, Gondo, Bow-wow, Furrs. Now *Beak*.

It had been Daddy Ronnie's nickname—"Beak Burk"—because his nose had been knocked haywire in football.

The guys Tommy hung out with weren't true hell-raisers, not in the sense of being brawlers. I knew each of them to have a soft side. But they presented themselves as tough. Before giving themselves nicknames, they'd called each other by their last names: Feaster, Bowden, Blevins, Fuller, Coppedge, Odom, Kelly, Stroope, English, Dorsett, Gordon, Walters, Sawyer, Wilson. A few of them lived in the country and had "hardship" drivers licenses, so they could drive legally. One night that fall, all thirteen of them piled onto a long flatbed truck to venture out toward misdeeds. Somehow they laid their hands on a discarded toilet and loaded it onto the truck. They left it sitting on Coach Joe Moore's front lawn, with a note attached: "Happy Crapping, the Commode Clan."

Suddenly, girls weren't just riding their bikes by our house anymore. They were coming onto our porch and ringing the doorbell.

In football, I was the weaker brother. The skinny one—the split end, not the tight end. Tommy's eighth grade teammates seemed like men compared to my seventh grade friends.

One weeknight in midseason, Dad came home from work early and drove me to my game at the junior high. We were talking about nothing in particular when he reached over and gave me a strong pat on my leg.

"You know what, Scotty," he said, "you're really strong."
What?
His words surprised me. I looked up at him.
Suddenly I felt alone with my father, for the first time. *Dad. Daddy Robert.* Up to then, he'd been a large component of our family—yet a virtual stranger to me. Now, as he drove us down Ross Street toward my game, I saw us as a combination of two. Not he and Mom, or he and Buzzy, or he and Tommy. *He and I.* It scared me—and thrilled me.

"You really are strong, Scotty," he said. "You're wiry."

Something surged in my veins. *He believed.*

With an oversized helmet atop my birdlike frame, I must have looked like a Tootsie Pop on the football field. But given those few simple words, I was set loose with a fury. On the Lancaster Tigers.

There was terror across the line of scrimmage. I could see it in the eyes of the player who lined up in front of me. He didn't know I was more than just skinny—I was *wiry*. He had no idea I'd had hands laid on me—that I'd been anointed for this battle. That I had a license to actually *kill* him—because my dad had said so.

For four quarters, my opponent felt the full force of ageless patriarchal blessing smashing against him—raging, punishing, delivering.

On the sidelines, my coaches pointed at me and grinned.

The next summer, Tommy and Darrell worked out harder, more seriously. They were about to enter high school. A buzz was going around about their freshman team, and the coaches had high expectations.

Meanwhile, I sought their advice on which teachers to take in eighth grade. Tommy said to be sure to take Mr. Hancock for history, because he had a sense of humor. Plus, he sometimes let you out of class early to work out or lift weights.

"Billy-Ray-Han-cock," Tommy said. He pronounced it fast, the way he used to say *Pepecek.*

"There's one thing you have to do in Mr. Hancock's class," Darrell said. "Call him 'Billy Frog.'"

"He loves it," Tommy said.

Nobody ever called a teacher by his first name. Much less by some dubious nickname. Why on earth would Mr. Hancock like this?

"He just does," Tommy said. "I'm telling you, do it. You'll get in good with him."

I tried it. Our class was taking a test, and I needed Mr. Hancock to clarify a question for me. I walked to his desk, leaned down and whispered.

"Excuse me, Billy Frog," I whispered. "Which Revolution is this question about?"

Mr. Hancock lifted his head slowly. He had a look of mild shock.

"It's about the Industrial Revolution," he said. *"Sawyer."*

I noticed him watching me all the way back to my seat. Maybe I'd shocked him by breaking the secret code, whatever it was. Maybe this meant I was getting in good with him.

When class ended, I made sure I stopped by his desk to ask about an assignment. "Uh, Billy Frog, could you–"

"Sawyer," he stopped me, "you call me that one more time, and the *frog will be hoppin'.*"

His anger took me aback.

In the hall, I asked a classmate what the frog was.

"Mr. Hancock's paddle," he answered.

If I'd learned to be wary of Tommy's lore, it didn't stop him from passing it along.

"Whatever you do," he advised, "don't get in trouble. Mr. Dorsey's got a paddling machine." He was talking about Harold B. Dorsey, the junior high principal at the time.

A what?

"A butt-whuppin' machine," Darrell specified.

"Three licks for a quarter," Tommy noted.

I rolled my eyes. How'd it work?

"He tells you to step up to this platform," Tommy said, "and he drops a quarter into this machine. Then a steel rod slowly raises up behind you, with a board screwed onto it."

"It's wrapped with tape," Darrell noted about the board. "And Old Weird Harold has drilled holes in it."

"When it raises up all the way, suddenly it goes off," Tommy said–*"pop-pop-pop."*

I laughed at the unlikely sequence. Bull, I said. What was Harold B. doing all this time?

"He's sitting there reading a magazine," Darrell said.

"While you're getting your tail whupped," Tommy pointed out.

Ridiculous! I said. Why would Mr. Dorsey waste a quarter on something he could just as easily do himself?

"He doesn't use quarters," Tommy reversed. "He just puts washers in it."

I hadn't yet gone to sleep when I heard tapping on the window. It was Darrell.

"Little Beak," he whispered. "Where's your brother?"

I peered into the dark. Tommy was sitting on the couch, tying his sneakers.

"Where are y'all going?" I said.

"Nowhere," Tommy whispered.

I sat up.

"Man, tell me."

"Shut up." He didn't look up. His mind was elsewhere.

I threw back the covers. "Let me go with you," I said.

"You're not going anywhere," he said.

"Come *on.*"

"You're not going, idge."

He tiptoed toward the back door, creaked it open, and closed it behind him.

I stood and looked out the side window. They were jumping over the brick wall at the side of our house.

I threw on my pants, shirt, and sneakers. They were probably headed down Ross Street, toward the junior high.

I sneaked out behind them, pushing the screen door quietly into place. I circled around the back of the house, jumped the brick wall, and started down Ross.

No sign of them. It was darker than usual—no stars out.

Then they appeared. They showed up under a streetlight, way down near Kirven Street. I took off in a jog. I couldn't figure out how they'd made it that far, that fast.

Everything was dead quiet in the neighborhood. After I'd run a block, I realized my sneakers were slapping the pavement loudly. I slowed down.

I kept looking for them to appear under the next streetlight, past Kirven. They didn't. I picked up my pace a bit, still trying to keep quiet. They still hadn't appeared. Now my breathing got loud. Where were they?

When I came to Kirven, I knew I'd missed them. They'd turned down some street, one with no light.

I jogged to the next block. I looked both ways down the street. It was all too dark. They were gone.

10

Tommy had become an option. When his freshman teammates lined up on offense, he was as likely to touch the ball as any of them. And he did. He caught everything Darrell threw near him. And most of it came to him in the end zone. Beak, the slow-footed tight end, ended up leading the team in scoring. In fact, he led the entire district.

Everybody knew Darrell was going to play varsity the next year. Not many sophomores got to do that. The surprise came when Waxahachie's head coach, Jack Moss, called Tommy. "Sawyer, I want you ready," he said. "You're going to play varsity ball next year."

We were discussing Tommy's promotion over dinner one night with Dad and Mom's friends, Grant and Sandy Matthews.

"Varsity, huh?" Grant mock-sniffed.

"Yes, sir," Tommy answered.

Grant turned to Dad. "Bobby, you ever seen a decent Waxahachie team since we played?"

"Oh, Grant," Mom groaned.

Grant asked Tommy what position he was going to play.

"Tight end," Tommy answered.

"Tight *end?*" Grant shook off an apparent chill. "They're gonna let you play tight end *again?*"

Tommy grinned.

"I look down there last year," Grant said, "and there's Wilson back in the pocket, scrambling all over the place. Then I look down and see Sawyer—*loping* across the end zone. Wilson's already crisscrossed the field twice. And there Sawyer is, *still* trying to make it across the end zone."

We all laughed.

"Finally, Wilson throws the ball. Perfect lead—*perfect*. But Sawyer's so slow, he has to *dive* for it. He even *comes down* slow."

Grant shook his head. "So, tell me, Sawyer," he said, "been working on your speed, have you?"

He pointed to the synthetic knee brace Tommy was wearing. Tommy's leg had started to get sore a few weeks after the season ended. The doctors said he'd probably been working out too hard.

Grant squinted at him skeptically. "You gonna catch anything this year?"

"I hope so."

"Well, you gonna do anything with it once you catch it?"

He glared at Tommy, then turned to me, incredulous. "Tight *end?*"

I kept wondering when they were going to let Tommy play. He stood on the sidelines during the varsity's spring practices and scrimmages, walking around stiffly in the knee brace. He got more somber with every passing week. Each doctor he'd seen had a different opinion.

Every day, after classes ended, Tommy waited for Mom in the high school library. When she'd wrapped up her class work and came down the hall to get him, she saw him reading. His head was bent down into the books, studying intently. Mom finally asked what he'd been reading about all that time.

"Cancer," he said.

He had known what was going to happen. Of course, there's no way he could have known, really. But somehow he had.

When the time came to tell Tommy what was wrong with his knee—that the leg brace hadn't done any good—Dad couldn't do it. The knot on his knee was cancer, and it was growing. They were going to have to cut off his leg.

Dad and Mom sat by his bed at the Methodist Hospital in Dallas. They'd taken him there for the doctors' final word. Now, just as Dad started to give Tommy the news, his voice cracked.

Our father cried. He wept and couldn't stop. He had to turn away.

Mom remained calm. She had to tell Tommy what was going to happen.

Osteogenic sarcoma—bone cancer. A twenty-percent survival rate, if they acted quickly enough.

Mom stayed at the hospital with Tommy that night, for the early surgery the next morning. Dad drove Buzzy and me home to Waxahachie. We didn't know what to think. We were silent for a while. Then, finally, we asked Dad questions. His replies were warm, calming.

"When you see Tommy tomorrow, he's not going to have his leg," he warned gently. "But I don't want you to worry about it."

"What are they going to do with it?" Buzzy asked.

"With what, honey?" Dad asked.

"With Tommy's leg."

Buzzy looked scared.

"I don't know, honey. But you don't have to worry about something like that. Okay?"

Buzzy's eyes were still wide.

"Are they going to bring it home?" he asked.

I expected to be hit with heaviness the next day when we walked into Tommy's hospital room. Just the opposite—the room was filled with flowers and laughter. Tommy was surrounded by his friends, the Commode Clan. They'd skipped school to be with him. They were all joking, as usual, and he was joking back. And there were a lot of girls in the room—girls I'd heard him and Darrell talking about.

That week, some of the Dallas Cowboys phoned Tommy. Roger Staubach talked to him for a long time. But Tommy was too shy to say much. He just answered, "Yes, sir," every once in a while. Other Cowboys sent autographed pictures with well wishes. Mike Ditka, who'd been traded to Dallas, wrote Tommy an encouraging letter. He advised my brother, "We old tight ends have to stick together."

We called it his stump. His left leg now ended at mid-thigh.

"You'll feel something called phantom pains," Dr. Berry, the surgeon, explained. "When we cut into your muscles, we couldn't just leave them hanging. We had to tie them up at the ends. So you may feel like your leg is still there, when it's not."

Phantom pains.

Tommy had to rub the stump constantly. It felt as if his leg had gone to sleep, he said, but he couldn't stretch it out to wake it up. It kept him leaning forward in his chair, rocking. At night, as we lay in our beds, he thudded the stump against the mattress, again and again, for hours. On some nights, Dad took him out driving, talking with him into the late hours, just to lull Tommy's mind and keep him from thinking about it. Yet no matter what they did, Tommy couldn't get his leg to wake up.

He had to walk on crutches for a couple of weeks, while his stump healed. He hadn't gone back to school yet. Mom realized it had been a long time since he'd been out in public, around people he didn't know well. She asked if he'd like to go to the grocery store with her.

"Yeah," he said.

They were aware of every head turning, every eye staring.

Then Mr. Wyatt, the store manager, saw them and waved. "Hey, partner," he said.

"Hi," Tommy said. He smiled.

One by one, the women they saw greeted them. "Hi, Pat," they said. "Hello, Tommy." They put a hand on his arm, or patted his shoulder. A few hugged him. Their eyes told him that nothing had changed, that he was still the same Tommy to them.

As Mom completed her shopping, they turned a corner onto the last aisle. A mother stood scanning the shelves, her small son beside her.

The boy's eyes trained on Tommy. He stared at the stump.

All the way down the aisle, Mom and Tommy felt the boy's stare. Finally, as they came near, the little boy looked into Tommy's face.

Tommy stopped. He lifted a crutch, aimed it at the child, and spouted, "*Rat-tat-tat-tat-tat-tat.*"

The boy laughed.

When his stump had healed, Tommy was fitted for a prosthesis. He walked slowly on the leg at first. He had to lift his hip high and swing the leg slightly outward. That way, the fake foot wouldn't drag the ground and cause him to fall. Sometimes it did, though, and he fell forward, crashing hard. He quickly learned to exaggerate his hip-lift—*quick step*, slow swing...*quick step*, slow swing ...

He came back to school wearing the prosthesis. The first time I saw him with his friends, it was disorienting. They were all walking along coolly, uniformly, as they always had. Only now Tommy was a sort of hitch in the line. He bobbed while they strutted. He had to swing his leg out slowly—unable to break into a run, as they'd often done before. Now his friends waited for him.

He finally went to the football field house, where his teammates were getting dressed for practice. One of the coaches was a sarcastic guy. He asked Tommy if he wanted to be a manager. "You know, Sawyer," he joked, "washing jocks, rounding up balls."

Legs

When I heard about this, I imagined Tommy laughing politely. I thought, didn't this guy know squat? Everybody knew Tommy wasn't going to be a manager.

When the weather got warm, he and Darrell drove out to the country club lake. They took off their shirts and shoes and got in the water. I don't know which of them suggested it, but they decided to swim across the lake. They made it all the way without stopping.

When Mom told me about this, I was suprised. I'd never even thought about attempting it. It was too far to risk, in my mind. Yeah, Tommy had always been a good swimmer, I thought. But that good? What made him do it?

I grew taller than my brother that summer. Still skinnier, but with an inch or two more height. I wondered if he'd stopped growing when they cut off his leg.

Football season came.

Tommy tried going to one of the varsity games with some of his friends. It was October, and the weather was cold and windy. His prosthesis was uncomfortable that day, so he decided to go on his crutches. He sat in the stands with his friends, yelling insults at the other team, joking about everything.

Sometime before the half, he got up to go to the men's room. As he stood in the aisle, however, he lost his balance. He fell backward—and he didn't stop. His crutches went flying. He kept rolling down, step after step.

Everyone rushed to help. Hands grabbing him, arms lifting him. All eyes on him.

79

Mom was nearby. When she finally got to him, he whispered to her, "Please get me out of here."

One afternoon, Mom was driving us home from school. I was in the front seat, Tommy in the back. We both were in a bad mood. I don't remember why. But we were going at each other again, just like the old days—not in a good way.

"Both of you, stay quiet till we get home," Mom said. She was trying to head something off.

But our barbs kept escalating. We couldn't help ourselves. Something was eating at us, something different in each of us.

I don't know what happened, exactly. Maybe when he swung open his door, it hit me. Or maybe I said one last word to him—one word too many, not willing to give him the last one.

I honestly don't remember who swung first. I only know I swung, and it landed. And I took off, instinctively, just as I'd always done.

I'd run five or six yards when he called me a name.

I stopped.

My mother sat with me in the living room, watching me shake as I cried.

"Please, honey," she said, "tell me what's wrong."

Tommy was at the back of the house, in our bedroom.

"What's he going to do when he goes to college?" I said. "What's he going to do then?"

She knew this wasn't what worried me. What worried me was, *Who's going to love him? Who's going to see my brother the way I see him—the way you see him, Dad sees him, his friends see him—not just as a cripple? What girl is going to look past his prosthesis, into who he is, the same way she'd look at anybody else?*

Sometime later, I was in the hallway between classes when I saw Tommy ahead of me. His back was to me. He was with his friends, casually walking along.

I noticed he wasn't swinging his leg out anymore. He strode smoothly. Now his movement seemed to be instinctive. Rhythmic. There was a slight hitch, but it was barely discernible. Almost normal.

11

Something had shown up on an X-ray. We were at the Methodist Hospital again, where they'd taken off Tommy's leg. The doctors had to perform surgery on his lungs to see what was there.

It was Thanksgiving Day, and it was just us, our family. The lobby was dark and cavernous and there weren't many people in it. We were going to be there for a few hours. Buzzy and I didn't talk much. We occupied ourselves by sliding an object back and forth across the slick tile floor, hockey style. Mom and Dad made an occasional phone call.

The surgeon was a big man, with large hands. His light blue cap fit tightly on his head. His mask was down as he approached us.

He spread out his arms to Mom and Dad. "I've got good news and bad news," he said. He took each of them under an arm. "The good news is, we don't have to take out his lung." He looked at Mom, then at Dad. "The bad news is, it's spread to his diaphragm and other areas. We can't operate on those."

Mom sunk her head into Dad. She wept.

That was it. That was the news.

Dad put his arms around Mom. He stroked her as the surgeon talked to them about options. Buzzy and I sat back down.

Tommy would be asleep for another few hours. Mom stayed at the hospital while Dad took Buzzy and me to get something to eat. As we walked across the parking lot, our father shook his head in disgust. "What in the world was good about any of that news?"

They had to drive Tommy to Houston—to M. D. Anderson, the cancer hospital. Dad would take a Friday off from work, and he and Mom drove the station wagon with Tommy riding in the backseat. Our brother received chemotherapy treatments that night and the next day, and they drove back on Sunday. During the drive home, Tommy threw up continually, then for nearly a week afterward. Mom sat with him in the backseat and held a pail for him.

Every morning, I noticed a new thatch of hair on Tommy's pillow. After a while, he lost almost all of it. His scalp began to look soft, like a baby's. At some point, Mom and Dad bought him a wig. It sat awkwardly on his head. He learned to adjust it, and over time we got used to it.

Buzzy was going back to Poppy and Ween's house after school, where he stayed until suppertime. I usually went to Big John's house. He had a hoops goal that was regulation height. We were about the same size, so we matched up well. We played endless games of one on one, sometimes till dark. Every basket counted as two, and the first guy to twenty won, only you had to win by four. So our games often extended well into overtime. Our tournaments did too, which were usually best four out of seven, five out of nine, even six out of eleven, just to keep going. We spent the whole afternoon dropping pound after pound of sweat. Shooting jumper after jumper, bank after bank, marking spots and aiming for the orange square. Focusing on the lines for guidance.

Every time they returned from a Houston trip, Tommy seemed different from before. He talked more easily with Dad and Mom, as if he were closer to their age than mine. On one trip, Mom took him between treatments to see *American Graffiti.* They brought back the eight-track tape of the soundtrack. Suddenly, Tommy knew all of Mom and Dad's old fifties songs. He also played an eight-track Dad had bought for him—Chuck Berry's *London Berry Sessions,* with the song "My Ding-A-Ling."

That Christmas, my present from Tommy was Elton John's *Goodbye Yellow Brick Road.* It was a double tape.

"That's the most expensive present your brother has ever bought anybody," Mom whispered to me. She wanted to connect something between us that she thought might be getting lost.

On New Year's Day, Tommy got to stand on the sidelines at the Cotton Bowl. The Longhorns' coach, Darrell Royal, had heard about him and sent him two sideline passes. Tommy asked Graham Compton to go with him. Graham was Mom's former student—the one in *Our Town* who'd strutted around backstage, giving everybody directions. Since then, Graham had undergone surgery for throat cancer. Now he'd fought it off.

As our family watched the game on TV, we saw Tommy and Graham standing on the Longhorns' sideline. It was a bitterly cold day, and they were trying to keep warm. Graham shifted from foot to foot. Tommy was on his crutches, without his prosthesis. He could only bunch his shoulders against the cold.

The Longhorns got drilled by Nebraska. Tommy and Graham ended up coming home early.

The winter dark began in late afternoon. By four o'clock, the lowering sun blared harshly through our bedroom window, blinding me. By five, it was dark.

The chemo Tommy received was dehydrating him. It grew worse with every trip. Now, toward the end of his weeklong sickness, he heaved with nothing to throw up. His body was getting weaker, taking longer to recover from each treatment. He was sick or weak most of the time, lying in bed or on the sofa in our room.

His friends weren't coming by as much anymore. Only Darrell visited from time to time. But he wasn't able to come as often because of varsity basketball.

Legs

I spent most afternoons that winter on the floor of our room, playing a football board game Dad and Mom had given me for Christmas. It was made up of a cylinder you rolled to determine each play from scrimmage, to see how far a gain you made. Some days, I rolled it the entire afternoon.

Mom told me that Tommy kept wanting to come to one of my basketball games. But he just couldn't. Whenever the time came, he was too sick.

One night we were playing DeSoto at home. I looked up, and there he was—sitting near the top of the bleachers with Dad and Mom. He was on crutches. His prosthesis had become too much trouble because of his pain.

I was aware of him the whole time. I played as if his eyes were on me, as if I were on some closed-circuit TV only he could watch. I scored four in the first half—two on a bank shot.

After the half, I'd forgotten they were there. When I looked up in the third quarter, they were gone.

He couldn't hold down water anymore. He spent the whole week throwing up, with nothing to put back in.

He finally told Mom no more. He had to stop.

They'd known it was killing him. So they stopped.

Mom wrote to cancer doctors—in New York, San Francisco, London. Sooner or later, they all wrote back. Some of their responses were clinical and cool, others warm and personal. They all said the same thing.

four

Eyes

12

SOMEONE HAD GIVEN TOMMY A TINY GOLD BOX FOR CHRIST-mas. He kept his pain pills in it. Every day he was having to pop them more often.

Mom had always trusted her eyes. To see what was important, what was needed, what could be given—to her family, her friends, her students. But how can you see anything, when there's nothing before you?

She remembered graffiti. Black Magic Marker she'd seen on a bathroom wall, at some roadside stop in Kansas, on the trip to pick me up. Simple words: "One Way."
She asked a friend about it—Iris Wilson, Darrell's mother.
"It's about Jesus, Pat," Iris said.

Stirring.

What about Jesus? she asked. What did she have to know about
him? How did she find it out?

"Just ask him," Iris said.

Lights.

Beams bouncing off metal fixtures. Filling the room with light,
eye-opening brightness. And filling her. Lifting her body
upward. Floating her, toward the ceiling—holding her there,
above everything. Above family, friends, students. Above cancer. Beaming inside her, making her warm.

She called Dad at work. She had to tell him about this.

She'd closed the door to the bathroom, she said, knelt at the
sink and prayed to Jesus. And he came to her. Full of light, lifting her up, physically, from the floor—

Dad listened.

"He was so real, Robert. I can't tell you—"

"Just, ah," he said, "just wait till I get home, sweetheart."

Then my father's face shone too. His smile—like none I'd ever
seen on him. The corners of his eyes, not hampered, not held
down by the day to day, by *anything.* His eyes—open, welcom-
ing. *Love.*

*As the words of [a] "Wanted" poster from a Christian underground
newspaper demonstrate, Jesus is alive and well and living in the . . .
spiritual fervor of a growing number of young Americans. . . . Their message: the Bible is true, miracles happen, God really did so love the world
that he gave it his only begotten son.*

—Time, *June 21, 1971*

Our parents drove us past the city limits on a road I hadn't remembered traveling. The Sturgeons' house was in a new edition, somewhere in the country. As we got out of the car, we heard voices from inside the house. Singing.

Tommy was on his crutches. He was in pain, and Mom and Dad had to help him out of the backseat. I followed them into the house.

The singing.

Twenty people stood in the living room—singing loudly, openly, arms lifted. Abandoned to something.

I knew. I knew. *I knew.*

It was *Him. He* was there.

There, in that man's face. In faces lifted upward, eyes shut. In lips whispering. *In the singing.*

Love.

Not a feeling—*a presence.*

It made me not want to speak. I felt heavy. Yet free.

I looked at everyone—sitting, standing, kneeling. People my parents' age, some older. Some faces familiar, others not.

Smiles that were—*tomorrow.* That were *yesterday, today, tomorrow*—the meaning of all things, rolled into one space—one house, one roomful of people, on one night.

He had come to us.

My parents—lifting their hands, their faces, their gladness at this—at *Him.*

My brother—his eyes closed, pain on his brow. Praying. *He knew.*

Everything new. Yet *there*, all along. *Here*—for us. *Now.*

The mountains skipped like rams,
The hills like lambs.
All the trees of the wood rejoice before the Lord:
for he cometh . . .

Mom was driving Buzzy and me to J. C. Penney, to buy us some basketball shoes. We asked her about these new things.

What is it okay to pray for?

"Anything," Mom said.

We pondered this. I was afraid of what to ask for. I aimed low. "Should I ask him to take the scar off my leg?" I said.

"Oh, honey," Mom said, "I think that would be 'putting God to a test.'"

"What does that mean?"

"It means asking him to do something he doesn't need to do. Anyway, your scar's a sign that God *does* heal."

Bonnie Hunt had been healed. She'd been going blind, and the doctors couldn't help her. So she went to people who prayed for her—and she was healed, completely. She had perfect vision. Now she came to the meetings at the Sturgeons' house.

But how, exactly, was she healed? I wondered. What did God do? What happened *inside her eyes?* Did new capillaries grow or something? Or did her blind spots just disappear?

. . . and he healed them (Matthew 4:24).
. . . and healed all that were sick (8:16).
. . . and great multitudes followed them, and he healed them all
(12:15).

. . . and he healed him (12:22).
. . . and he healed their sick (14:14).
. . . and he healed them (15:30).
. . . and he healed them there (19:2).
. . . and he healed them (21:14).

"And hope does not disappoint."

Hope.

The minister closed his Bible. Music started.

He motioned to my parents, to come forward. There was a healing service in Dallas, he said.

Some men showed up at our house in a van, men we didn't know. They all had kind faces. Dad helped them put Tommy onto a portable stretcher and load it into the van. Then Dad climbed into the passenger seat, and Mom and I climbed into the back. We sat on the shag carpet, next to Tommy's stretcher.

My brother was in pain, so we kept our voices low. The men whispered as they spoke with Mom, smiling and nodding occasionally. Mom stroked Tommy's hand as she talked.

The auditorium in Dallas was large. Inside was a wide, open space, with dozens of rows of folding chairs. People sat scattered throughout the space, in small patches of groups. We entered from the back. The men from the van rolled Tommy's stretcher to the back row.

The minister was already speaking when we arrived. He was Australian. He spoke for half an hour or so, walking back and forth across the stage. His voice was gentle, reasonable. When he finished, he asked people to come forward, one by one, forming a single-file line at the foot of the stage.

The men and women who stood in line were mostly older. They had back ailments, limps, vision problems. The minister spoke softly into the microphone as he prayed for each of them, one after the other. Each time, the person he prayed for said he could feel something happening. Something warm, not big or dramatic.

Suddenly, we heard a low roar. It came from the left side of the auditorium. The people sitting in that area had been stirred. Now they were shouting, getting louder.

The minister stopped praying. He peered out to where the commotion was taking place. The people there were crying out things. One woman fell to her knees. A man stood and raised his arms in praise. More arms went up. More cries, more praises.

Dad motioned to the men who'd come with us. They each grabbed a side of Tommy's stretcher and began wheeling it toward the noisy area. They had to move slowly, because of Tommy's pain.

It seemed to take them forever. I watched them navigate the pathways between the rows of chairs. First, a long stretch. Then a left turn. Another long stretch. A right turn. Finally, down the long, open walkway along the building's left side.

By the time they arrived, the people had quieted down. They were all on their knees. Praying softly, wiping tears. Thanking God for what had happened.

It was over.

The auditorium had emptied. We waited in a long hallway, where we were told the minister would come out. We'd been there for half an hour when we saw him. One of the men from the van was walking alongside the minister, pointing to us.

The minister had a warm, open face. He listened quietly as Mom and Dad explained to him about Tommy's cancer. Then he stepped to my brother's side.

"Let me ask you, Tommy," he said, "do you want to be healed?"

Tommy was in pain. He nodded.

"I know you do, son," he said. "We just want to state that before the Lord, in agreement together, to affirm our desire to him. Please—" he motioned to everyone, to gather around Tommy's stretcher—"let's all agree before the Lord."

I looked at my brother.

Let it happen.

The minister began praying. Everyone joined in, praying aloud.

I closed my eyes—prayed, listened.

Voices surrounding my brother. Praising. Asking, pleading. Voicing gratitude. Desire. Challenge.

Then, a thought dropped like a lead weight:

No—it won't.

My eyes shot open. I shut them again, quickly—tightly. Against doubt. Against reason.

Let it happen.

Five minutes. Everyone still praying, loudly.

Now I looked.

My brother—his eyes open, face in pain. On his back, looking toward the ceiling. In agony. By himself.

Let it happen.

But—

What would it look like?

Shut my eyes again.

Everyone praying—crying now. Louder. Sadder. Bolder.

Ten minutes.

Would we see him gain weight? Grow hair? Get up from the stretcher? Walk around?

On one leg?

The minister wouldn't give up.

Every person pleading. Heads lowered, determined. Not letting up.

Fifteen minutes.

I don't have to imagine what it looks like. That's doubt. Don't doubt!

I looked again. Looked at Tommy's chest, leg, eyes. Was it happening, and we didn't know it?

No.

Twenty minutes.

We stopped.

The drive home was slow. Quiet in the van.

I heard Dad whispering to the driver.

"If we just could've gotten him down there," he said. "If we could've gotten him there when God was still healing."

The pain pills were virtually useless now. Mom called Dr. Fearis to see if he could give Tommy anything stronger. He came to our house and gave Tommy a shot of morphine. Within minutes Tommy was in agony—he was having an allergic reaction. He felt like fire ants were in his body.

Dr. Fearis told Mom he would try to find some stronger pills.

What if he was healed? I wondered. What if God took away all the cancer? What if Tommy's body miraculously went back to the way it was?

I thought about it, to myself.

We wouldn't be the same. People wouldn't allow it. They would come to our house just to ask about the healing. Strangers who didn't know Tommy or us. They would want him to speak at their churches, their meetings. But he wouldn't know any of them, and neither would we. He'd be on the news. A freak. A *thing.*

And *he* would have to be different. His buddies wouldn't know what to think of him. He'd have to have a whole new set of friends, made up of strangers, people who weren't really like him. They wouldn't know him deep down—not as he really was.

Would I still know him?

13

Mom hadn't taught school at all that year. She was at home with Tommy every day. The school board had voted to pay her salary anyway.

Her back had always been weak. Whenever she'd tried to move heavy things, she'd ended up in bed for days. Now she was carrying my brother to the bathtub every day, to clean him.

"Jesus healed me, Scotty," she said.

I believed her.

I wasn't sleeping in the back bedroom anymore. I'd moved into the adjacent one. Now Mom stayed in the back with Tommy, in case he needed something during the night.

I didn't go into our old bedroom much anymore. When I did, my brother made eye contact with me briefly, but he seemed to look past me. I'd be home after school, maybe looking for something in a drawer. He'd be lying on his bed, in pain—his skin yellow, his head often moving from side to side, like a vein throbbing.

He was in a different world. Different from all of ours, except maybe Mom and Dad's. How could he ever come back from this? I thought. How would his friends, the people who loved him, ever see him the same again?

I'd stopped trying to imagine it.

I knew his friends still cared. Every day at school, at least one of them asked me, "How's Tommy doing?"

"Fine," I said.

Since he'd stopped chemotherapy, his hair had begun growing back in. It was short, coming in uniformly like a crew cut. Because everybody else had long hair, it made Tommy look like a kid again. He looked even more childlike as he lay in bed—his shirt off, his chest thin, his arms thin.

Mom sat with him throughout the day, talking to him, encouraging him. She seemed to *see* again—to *hope*. To know what to say and do, in spite of everything.

"Jesus is here, Tommy," she said. "He's with us, right now."

One afternoon I sat in the room with them playing a new tape I'd bought. It was a Beatles anthology—the blue one, their later stuff. The tape clicked onto "All You Need Is Love."

"You remember that old Beatles song, Tommy?" Mom said. "All you need is Jesus, honey. He's all any of us needs."

Tommy glanced at her, listening. He didn't say anything.

I knew the music was a little too loud. But I didn't want to turn it down. I just wanted to enjoy my new tape.

"Scotty, please, honey," Mom said. "Can you turn that down a bit?"

He finally had a good day. He wasn't in as much pain, and he felt talkative. Mom wanted to record some of his thoughts in her diary, so she took dictation while he spoke.

"What I would really like to do," he told her, "would be to have my leg back, be six feet three, weigh 220 pounds, and be a tight end for a pro football team. Play a game on real grass, on a kind of muddy field, a day after it rained. I love the competition of the whole team working together as a unit—each man doing his job, so all the plays run just like clockwork. And I love the rivalry of it. I love everything Vince Lombardi had to say about the game, because winning is everything to me."

What else?

"I'd want to be a writer."

"A writer," she wrote carefully.

"Yes."

They talked for another twenty minutes or so, until finally Mom began to put her journal aside.

"Mom?" Tommy stopped her.

"Yes, honey." She opened her diary again.

"Please don't stop praying for my friends."

I woke to his agonizing. It was some early hour. I raised my head and saw that the lamp was on in the back bedroom.

He was gargling out pain. His lungs no longer had the strength to yell in protest.

I heard Mom opening the pill box. I knew she was lifting his head from the pillow and a glass of water to his lips. Then I heard her praying over him gently, asking Jesus to stop the pain.

After a while, Tommy's moans became cries. Gargled cries, from the back of his throat.

Mom talked to him softly. I couldn't hear what she said.

I woke again.

The lamp was still on. He was still moaning.

"We've got Jesus, honey," I heard Mom say. "He's right here with you, Tommy. One of these days, we're all going to see Jesus defeat Satan for good."

She read to him.

How art thou fallen from heaven, O Lucifer, son of the morning! How art thou cut down to the ground, which didst weaken the nations! . . .

Thou shalt be brought down to hell, to the sides of the pit. They that see thee shall narrowly look upon thee, and consider thee, saying, Is this the man that made the earth to tremble, that did shake kingdoms; that made the world as a wilderness . . . ?

I was watching TV in the den. Mom peeked in. She had to go to Penney's, she said, to buy some track shoes for Buzzy. He had a Junior Olympics meet in two days. I would be alone here with Tommy.

"Don't worry, Scotty," she assured me. "I won't be gone long. No more than fifteen minutes."

No hurry, I thought.

I went to the back bedroom.

Tommy was in pain—numbing pain.

I sat down on the bed next to his—my old twin bed. I looked at my brother.

Something woke in me.

Tommy.

Not Tommy and us. Not Tommy and Mom. Tommy and me.

A terror hit me.

I realized I'd been sleepwalking through his pain—for weeks.

Now I saw it all. His bloated ankle. His body gone bony, his neck thin. His eyes sunken.

Tommy. My big brother, who looked like a child again. A soft stubble on his chin—his "man" whiskers, on a kid's body.

I couldn't speak. I didn't want to. Didn't want to show my ignorance, my blindness. My avoidance. Avoidance of what he'd been going through—of what he'd felt all that time, without me there to listen, or to say something.

His eyes were locked on the ceiling, his head moving back and forth. Finally, he glanced at me. Said nothing. Looked straight past me. Tossed his head again—wincing, making a low groan.

I didn't know how to help. What to ask.

He looked at me again—straight at me. His eyes boring through me, past me. To something I couldn't give.

Something was happening—something not normal.

Tommy raised his head as far as he could. His mouth opened.

A dark brown liquid came up out of him. It came up again. He threw up a gallon, maybe more. It splashed onto his chest, his stomach—ran down his thigh, his stump. It was thin, watery, trickling over his skin. It formed a pool under his body, where he sank into the mattress.

I froze. What was happening? Was he about to—

He moaned loudly.

I ran to the bathroom to get some towels.

Old towels—get old towels that won't get ruined.

Idiot! Don't worry about towels.

I ran back in, pressed a towel to Tommy's skin to wipe up the blood. He moaned. I drew back, thinking I might be hurting him. I tried again, pressing more softly.

I cleaned most of the blood from him. But he still lay in a deep pool of it. I grabbed fresh towels and pressed them onto the bed around him.

He moaned again. Maybe I'd bumped down on the mattress too hard. I tried pressing the towels more softly. The brown pool only seemed to rise higher around him.

He kept moaning.

I used towel after towel. Now they all were soaked.

Don't ruin them all.

Stupid idge—forget the towels!

Finally, I straightened up. I held all the blood-soaked towels.

Put them on his bed—it's already bloody.

No! Don't lay those filthy things next to your brother.

I kept holding the towels. I leaned back slowly and sat on the other bed.

He lay in the blood, while we waited for Mom.

She came. She'd only been gone ten minutes.

"Oh, no," she moaned to heaven. She sprang into action, knowing exactly what to do. She cleaned up the blood in a matter of minutes. Then she shifted Tommy, gently, to make him more comfortable. All the while, she was whispering things to calm me.

"I'm so sorry, honey," she said. "I knew the devil was going to try something while I was gone."

Tommy gazed upward, away from us, his head turning from side to side.

I stood by, mute. Why was she apologizing to me?

A day passed.

I woke to clanging noises. The kitchen light was on. It shone onto the carpet at the far end of my room, and into the hall. Something glowed there, something yellow.

It was Tommy's skin. Yellow in the light.

He was lying on a hospital stretcher, awake. His face was in pain. Yet he looked calmer than I'd seen him.

He was surrounded by people. Young guys, in white outfits. They were wheeling him out. I heard Mom whispering to them.

Fell back asleep.

We were working on an assignment in English class. Coach Lofland poked his head into the room and summoned our teacher, Mrs. Berryman. She stepped outside for a minute or so. The coach stuck his head back into the room and motioned to me.

They were standing together in the hallway. Mrs. Berryman was crying. She tried to smile. Coach Lofland spoke. "Your parents are at the hospital with your brother," he said. "They want you to go home with John today."

Big John and I were playing chess in the entrance hallway of his house. The doorbell rang. Before John could get up, my parents let themselves in. Mom had been crying.

I searched their faces.

"Scotty," Mom said, "Tommy's with Jesus."

Relief.

I lay my head on my forearms and shook.

My mother and father hugged me from behind.

"We've got to take care of some things, honey," Mom said. "Buzzy's with Ween and Poppy." She smiled at my best friend. "Do you want to go with us or stay here with John?"

"I'll just stay."

John sat in silence as I cried.

"Why don't we quit," he finally said. He meant chess.

"No," I said. "Let's keep playing."

Buzzy had his track meet that day. It was being held at the high school. John's mother drove us there. "Tommy would have wanted him to run," Mom had said.

Our little brother did run. It was a hurdle race, with half a dozen fifth-graders. Buzzy crossed the finish line first.

Sometime in the next few days, my parents told me how Tommy had died.

"They'd given him as much medication as they could," Dad said, "so he was in and out all day."

"Then, suddenly he looked up," Mom said. "He just came awake, but he didn't see us. He looked into one corner of the ceiling, as if he saw something there. Then he just closed his eyes. And his heart stopped beating."

What did he see?

Just outside the funeral sanctuary, Dad gathered us in a circle. He put one arm around my shoulder, the other around Mom's, with Buzzy in the midst of us. Beyond the doors sat all our friends. Tommy's body was in the casket at the front.

"I don't want you to be sad when we walk in there," Dad said. His words were for Buzzy and me. "That won't be Tommy up there. It's just an old shell."

Yes, we knew that. But it felt good to hear our father say it. When we walked in, though, and saw all our friends crying, heard the music, and saw Tommy, all the sadness rushed back in. We all cried—all except Dad. He kept his arms around us and led us to the front pew.

I don't remember the ride to the burial site. But I remember being there. At one point I turned and saw Uncle Dennis, Mom's brother. He was in his Air Force officer's uniform. He stood straight, at attention, with a dignity I'd rarely seen in anyone.

I glanced at Mom and Dad as they prepared to lower the casket into the ground. Dad was staring straight ahead—straight at the casket. Trying to see inside it. Trying to see Tommy one last time.

I saw his chin quiver. It was sending a silent message. *Goodbye.*

It was the last week of school, and Mom and I had just driven home after classes. We were about to walk in the house when she stopped. "Scotty," she said, "do you mind sitting with me out here for a minute?"

We sat on the porch swing. She put her face in her hands and began crying.

"I just miss him so much," she said. She let it all pour out.

I was silent as she cried.

"One day we're going to get to see Jesus throw Satan in the pit," she said. "Maybe then everybody who's suffered will get a chance to torment him, for all the things he did to them."

Our parents' Sunday school class took up a collection for us, so we could take a vacation. When school was out, we drove to Connecticut, to visit Mom's youngest sister, Aunt Dianne, and her family.

Eyes

Driving home, we took the eastern route, down the Blue Ridge Parkway in Virginia. On a quiet afternoon, as Dad drove, Mom gazed out the window. "Look," she said suddenly. "Look there, at that cloud. It's Tommy's face."

I couldn't find it.

"That cloud—right there, Robert. It's exactly the shape of Tommy's face."

She kept trying to point it out, but I couldn't see it. I never did.

Part II

five

Ghosts

Heavenly Father, we thank You that by water and
the Holy Spirit You have bestowed upon these Your
servants the forgiveness of sin, and have raised them
to the new life of grace. Sustain them, O Lord, in
Your Holy Spirit. Give them an inquiring and discerning heart, the courage to will and to persevere,
a spirit to know and to love You, and the gift of joy
and wonder in all Your works.

—The Book of Common Prayer

14

THE FIRST THING I MISSED ABOUT TOMMY WAS HIS VOICE. IT
might be his attempt at a whistle, or his laugh. Some sound I'd
listened to only indirectly—something I hadn't realized I was
taking for granted. Or maybe I just wanted to tell him something. I thought of a joke I knew only he would get. Or I
observed some quirky trait in someone that I knew only he
would think was funny. Yet, just as I turned my head and
opened my mouth to speak, my grief slapped me awake.

This happened within the first few days. Then, a week after his funeral, I woke up in a panic—I couldn't remember what his face looked like. It didn't matter that we had hundreds of pictures of him. My memory could no longer summon his image the way it once could. I knew something terrible was happening. And whenever I panicked about it, my memory blurred even more.

Not long after this, the dormant grief you tried so hard to push down surfaces. It's desperate to speak. There must be meaning from this, *it tells you. So you determine to find that meaning. One day, you have a revelation—you think maybe you've grasped what that big meaning is. It all has to do with God, and the grand design he had for your loved one's life, as well as yours.*

You start to voice this revelation. But with every word you speak, something in your memory diminishes. You can't go back now, you realize—you've already convinced yourself that this is the big meaning. So you continue to speak it, even though you grow more despairing with every telling.

Worse, every time you talk about your loved one, you remember him less as he really was. Your words don't do justice to the life, the person you once knew—instead, he's a caricature. You see that your words have given him a different shape, a different form, a different meaning. A different face. A different voice. A different existence. Now, every word you speak about him seems not just wasted, but cursed—falling to the ground the moment it leaves your tongue.

I dreamed about Tommy regularly, frequently. Every couple of days, I saw him alive again. Then it was every couple of weeks, and later months.

He was always looking away from me. He might be casually walking along with some of his friends, talking to them and not to me. We never had a direct conversation. I'd run alongside him, virtually tugging at his sleeve, asking, "Where have you been? And how could you be alive? I saw you lying there in the casket. I saw them lower it in the ground and put the dirt on top of it. How did you survive all that?"

He didn't pay much attention, and he never answered me directly. He might acknowledge me, but only in a dismissive sort of way—as if he were walking down Ross Street again with Darrell, trying to get away from me. My reaction was always bittersweet: he's alive, just as I knew he always was, and that's what counts. But another part of me had to know: What have you been doing? And what do you think about? Do you think about me, the way I always think about you?

My mother saw ghosts too.

Every rare once in a while, she glanced at me doing something unselfconsciously—say, lying on the floor reading, legs crossed at the ankles, wagging one foot rapidly, like a dog's limb shaking off water. The image caught her up short. For a moment, she saw lanky Daddy Ronnie again—stretched out on the living room floor of their crackerbox house in West Station, Texas, thumbing through a fishing catalog.

She never talked about Daddy Ronnie at length. I got only snatches. Snapshots, tossed out casually as they flashed in her mind.

She mentioned in passing that he'd liked the actress Yvonne DeCarlo.

Yvonne DeCarlo? That's Lily Munster. What on earth was he thinking?

Also, he and a buddy had acted out Martin and Lewis routines at their fraternity parties. Daddy Ronnie played Jerry Lewis.

What? How could this dark-eyed, serious guy act that goofy?

She said he sometimes signed his letters, "Wit." Short for *Witten*, his middle name.

I found one of his scrapbooks in a closet. As I thumbed through it, I came across some newspaper photos of Don Maynard, the receiver for the New York Jets. He and Daddy Ronnie had run in a track meet against each other. Maynard had smoked everybody.

"Why'd he keep these pictures of Don Maynard?"

"He kept clippings on people he admired," she said.

His two red-and-black coaching jackets had hung in a storage closet for years. When I tried them on, they both fit perfectly. One of them appeared almost new, having barely been worn.

By this time I had my own letter jacket—for basketball, in Waxahachie's forest green. One day, though, I decided to wear one of Daddy Ronnie's jackets to school. I wondered what people would think when they saw a red "W" on the front instead of a green one.

I had it on that afternoon at a baseball game, when the weather was still brisk. Mr. Dorsey, now the high school principal, noticed it as I walked by.

"West Station," he said wistfully, eyeing the red "W" on the front. "Ah, yes."

I was startled. Harold Dorsey knew about West?

Did he also know about my father?

I smiled and kept walking.

Daddy Ronnie's scrapbook had lain on the same closet shelf as Dad's. The two scrapbooks were equally thick. Now I took out Dad's and began thumbing through it. It yielded a few surprises of its own.

There was a picture of Dad in a *basketball* uniform. He'd played hoops—*my* game—as a freshman. He'd never mentioned a word about it.

"You never said you played basketball," I said over dinner one night. "You were on the freshman team."

He cocked his head and sniffed, à la Barney Fife. "High point against Forreston," he coughed. As if to say, *Didn't want to brag about it.*

"Oh, Robert," Mom moaned. "Don't listen to him, Scotty. He was never anything in basketball."

I checked out his claim: he had 21 against Forreston.

Then, I couldn't help myself—I secretly compared all our high point games:

Dad: 21.

Daddy Ronnie: 20.

Me: 19.

Sometimes I imagined what I might be doing on any particular day had Daddy Ronnie lived. Maybe push-ups or wind sprints. Maybe more chores. The Jerry Lewis factor notwithstanding, I thought of Daddy Ronnie as quiet, earnest, disciplined.

I knew this: Had he lived, I probably wouldn't have got my rear sprayed with air freshener, as Dad did when he happened by while spraying the house.

Occasionally, I got accused of Daddy Ronnie's stubbornness.

"He was *horrible,*" Mom shuddered. "Once I was ten minutes late to meet him for a date. *Ten minutes.* He didn't talk to me for three days."

I recognized the same upright tendency in myself. Could *personality* be transferred genetically? I didn't buy it.

"You're just like him," she assured me. "Parsimonious."

What's that?

"Conservative with money."

Wait a minute—I was a notorious spendthrift. I was always blowing my allowance on movies. They'd become my biggest vice. Every week I drove to Dallas impulsively, burning gas to see some new film I'd read about. And, invariably, I came up short of funds at the end of each week.

"Nah, I think you're pretty conservative," Mom said. "You may blow it, but at least you always know how much you have. Just like him."

Except for the nights when Ronnie was away scouting, my mother had loved being a coach's wife. The men enjoyed a boisterous camaraderie, and the wives loved throwing parties. They were all young, just getting started, with big dreams. Ronnie's was to be the head track coach at Rice University. He relished the thought of coaching at a pinnacle of higher learning.

Their newlywed naïveté revealed itself at the butcher shop in West. When they requested bologna, the butcher asked how much. They looked at each other and shrugged. "Ten pounds." When the massive slab came across the counter, they were too embarrassed to send it back.

She threw a "newlywed fit" every now and then. He reacted with legendary stubbornness. One weekend she left their small rented house, with Tommy in tow, and took a bus to Waxahachie, to stay with Nanny and Granddaddy. Nanny listened to her story. When Mom was finished, her mother would have none of it. "You get back there," Nanny said. "You're not a child anymore. You've got responsibilities."

Ronnie made her pray at night, something she'd never done. She secretly rolled her eyes. She'd been to church camp once, invited by an Episcopalian friend. All she'd learned to do there was dance and cuss.

We drove to Fort Worth every Sunday for church. It was a charismatic congregation, made up of some of the people who'd been with us through Tommy's cancer.

"The enemies of your faith," our pastor frequently taught: "doubt, fear, and unbelief."

He was less a preacher than a thorough teacher—extremely thorough. For years, he'd held a Friday night Bible study. When I joined the group as a teenager, they had just started studying the book of Revelation. Two years later, when I left for college, they'd progressed to chapter 9.

By contrast, my parents held informal Bible studies for teenagers every Wednesday night in our living room. The lessons were usually taught by Mom and Cleta Jones, a fellow English teacher and my mother's closest friend. Cleta had a strong theological background, having studied at Loyola in Chicago, as well as years of practical experience in the Salvation Army. Their lessons on Wednesday nights were mostly spiritual exhortations, punctuated with testimonies from daily life.

They also gave the teenagers a chance to teach. These lessons usually centered around spiritual zeal. Indeed, the text was often from the book of Acts, where Jesus' apostles—fresh from their moment of doubt and defeat, at the crucifixion—began performing amazing feats through the power of the Holy Spirit. Reading these accounts, we envisioned ourselves as part of a movement foreseen by the Old Testament prophet Joel: "Your young men will dream dreams, and your old men will see visions."

One night someone taught from the Sermon on the Mount, in Matthew's gospel. We read the passage where Jesus addresses fathers:

Which of you earthly fathers, if your son asks for bread, will give him a stone? Or if he asks for a fish, will give him a snake? If you, then, though you are evil, know how to give good gifts to your children, how much more will your father in heaven give good gifts to those who ask him!

The reading prompted a discussion on God's faithfulness. But I was indignant. How could Jesus say that all fathers are evil? I thought. How could he say *my* father was evil?

More and more, my peers spoke of receiving "revelations" from the Lord—moments when they suddenly realized something they couldn't have known otherwise. Occasionally, someone testified of having what might be considered a prophetic dream.

For example, they might be warned ahead of time about some incident that would take place, and the event later came to pass.

I didn't have such revelations. My only dreams were of my brother. *Why?* I prayed. *Why don't I dream about you, Jesus?* What had I done?

"Being baptized into his death," a friend of mine read. He stopped at this verse. "What does that mean, Mrs. Sawyer?"

How could he not know what this means? *Death, yes—no problem.* That's what it's all about, don't you see? That's the only way to be like Him—to identify with death. To *die now*—to give up your life, for all practical purposes. Doesn't anybody around here understand anything?

I couldn't comprehend why everybody prayed about things like boyfriends or girlfriends. How could they get bogged down in things as frivolous as that? Didn't they know what hung in the balance, every day of their lives?

I had nothing against dating. I did plenty of it. I even asked out a girl from Tommy's class—an old friend of his, someone he and Darrell used to talk about. We only went out a couple of times. I could tell she didn't enjoy being with me that much.

I didn't mind dropping it. It had felt strange, anyway. As if I'd been stealing something.

15

It was 1975, and the "410 English" courses at Waxahachie were part of an experimental program meant to involve kids in more than the standard English curriculum. The courses changed every six weeks. That year, Mom taught a perplexing range of subjects—from Dickens' *Great Expectations* to creative drama, in which the students themselves scripted and acted out scenes, to the Reverend David Wilkerson's *The Cross and the Switchblade*. How she got away with the last one, we could never figure out. It's a testimonial book written by a country preacher who helped New York City gang members kick their heroin habits by leading them to Christ. The probable justification for allowing the book in a public classroom was, "Anything to get kids to read."

I had Mom for a few courses that year. In one class, she teared up as she read A. E. Housman's poem, "To an Athlete Dying Young." Any power the poem had was lost on me. It was all about a community's reaction to a young guy's premature death. To me, it said nothing about what the athlete himself had been through.

Mom had always written poetry—for friends, family, fellow teachers, even for community events. One summer she read about a poetry contest that offered a sizable grand prize, and she and Cleta decided to enter. They were allowed to submit as many entries as they wanted, so every day they hammered out verse after verse. In the evenings, they traded their thickening sheaves to encourage each other.

Evidently, Dad was involved in some of the readings. One evening he pointed out that the quantity of output had begun to outweigh the quality.

"Oh, listen to Shakespeare," Mom retorted. To my shock, she began reciting something Dad apparently had written. "*Oh, how I love the smell of the grass when I go to the football field, Oh how I love to punt the ball . . .*"

Dad's flushed grin said it was at least partly true.

I love to punt the ball?

Nah—not *Dad*. How could it be?

I only wished I'd been there to witness the attempt.

Mom had always been a fairly reliable resource for me on movies. I'd never really talked with Dad about them. The only time I'd ever heard him refer to a movie was when he gamely imitated some actor.

Alan Ladd being menaced in *Shane:* "Ya speakin' ta me?"

Gary Cooper as a confused *Sergeant York:* "I don't rightly know..."

An embattled Marlon Brando in *One-Eyed Jacks:* "Yew scum-suckin' pig."

Whenever the weekly issue of *Time* arrived, Mom and I fought over who got to read it first—she, to scan news features for her debaters, I to pore over Jay Cocks' film reviews.

One night I was in my room, reading *Time*'s assessment of a new Ingmar Bergman film, *The Magic Flute*. This director was new to me. The review described him in reverent tones, mentioning a canon of work I'd never heard of. I wondered if the new film might be worth driving to Dallas to see.

I went to the den, where I found Dad leaning back on the sofa, watching TV.

"Where's Mom?" I asked.

"Had to go back to the school, for something or other."

I threw down the gauntlet.

"Ever heard of Ingmar Bergman?"

He glanced at me curiously, then quickly back at the TV.

"Yeah."

"What do you know about him?"

"Saw *Wild Strawberries* when I was at Texas."

Wild Strawberries? What on earth was that? And what had made *him* go see it? I couldn't imagine him lasting through a foreign movie.

"Did you like it?"

I braced for his patented eye-roll.

"Sure," he answered, without looking up. "It was all right."

The more I learned about Dad, the more incongruous I saw
him with his surroundings. He made his home in small-town
Waxahachie; he wore French cuffs to his workplace in Dallas.
Nobody ever accused Dad of being a snob, but the idiosyncra-
cies of some of our town's characters were rarely lost on him.

I sometimes accompanied him to the grocery store on Friday afternoons, when he wanted to cash a check for the weekend. He never failed to complain about the long line of people
ahead of him at the cashier's window.

"Must be rain coming," he said, shaking his head.

Why?

"Everybody's stocking up, afraid of getting flooded out."

He also had a compulsive need to be early, no matter where
he went. He was always up hours ahead of time before leaving
for work—taking care of chores, working a crossword puzzle, or
just sipping coffee, watching the hummingbirds zip around the
feeder in the backyard.

Mom found his compulsion tiresome. "Why do we always
have to be everywhere an hour ahead of time?" she complained.

"You never know," he answered. "Something could happen
on the way."

He poked fun at me whenever I came home from a rock con-
cert in Dallas or Fort Worth, wide-eyed and citing it as "the ultimate."

"They're *all* 'the ultimate,'" he said.

But, for my sixteenth birthday, he bought me tickets to see
Eric Clapton. Clapton had become my music hero—the guitarist
Tommy had listened to, second in stature only to the Beatles.

The loner, the calm figure onstage who closed his eyes soulfully when he soloed, shutting out the rest of the world.

I dreamed about Eric Clapton once too. He came into my room as I was getting ready for school. I watched in awe as he casually thumbed through some items on my desk. He must have known how much I admired him, how I'd longed to meet him. But how did he find his way to our house? And into my room, to me?

16

Before I left for college, Dad handed me a checkbook. He and Mom had opened an account for me at the bank. He also handed me a folded check made out to me. It was from a different bank.

"That's the college savings Daddy Ronnie started for you and Tommy," Mom explained. She'd told us about the account years before. At that time, the balance was around $2,000. I looked at the amount now: over $3,000.

It wasn't all mine, I thought. It was supposed to have been split.

"Should we save half for Buzzy?" I said.

"No, honey," Mom said. "It needs to go toward what it was set aside for."

A week after I left for Baylor, an hour away in Waco, Mom called.

"I've only seen your father cry twice in my life," she said. "The first time was when Tommy had to have his leg amputated. The other time was last week, as you were driving away."

I tried hard to imagine it.

Mom had given me Daddy Ronnie's graduation rings from high school and college. Sometime that year, I began wearing his ring from North Texas State. The metal was gold, with a green stone in the center. Across the stone, the Greek letters Sigma Phi Epsilon were embossed in gold.

I had the ring on during rush week, when I went to a Sig Ep party.

"Hey," one member pointed out, "you're a legacy."

"I guess so," I said.

Near midterm, I was up late studying for an exam. As I looked at my watch, for some reason the date leaped out: October 22.

I don't know how I had remembered the date or why it had occurred to me. But it had, and everything came back to me.

I set aside my study notes and started a letter to Dad. It turned out to be a long one. It was a thank-you to him for adopting Tommy and me.

A week later, I received a package in the mail. Inside was a thank-you note in return from Dad, along with a pair of Nikes.

Mom called afterward. "Well, that's the third time I've seen your dad cry," she said.

I was walking across campus on a Monday morning when I ran into a classmate from Dallas. He'd been home with his family over the weekend.

"Hey, Sawyer," he greeted me, "your mom's an awesome writer."

What?

"Didn't you see Sherrod's column? It's about your brother, man."

Which brother?

"Your brother who died. It was in the paper yesterday."

Somewhere on campus I picked up a copy of the *Dallas Times Herald*. Roger Staubach had retired. Mom had written to the sports columnist Blackie Sherrod, describing everything Staubach had done for Tommy. She hadn't wanted to miss the opportunity to honor him in return.

Mom and Dad brought Buzzy to Baylor with them for Parents' Weekend. We went out for dinner at a popular steak restaurant. As we were eating, Mom recognized a man walking across the room.

"That's Wade Turner," she said. "Wade!"

The man looked up. He had graying hair and a stocky build. Mom motioned to him.

"He was one of Daddy Ronnie's coaching friends," she said. I didn't look at Dad. I just kept eating.

The man came toward our table.

"Wade, I'm Pat," Mom said. "Remember? Ronnie Burk's wife."

"Pat, how are you?" he said. He had a cordial manner. "It's so good to see you." He quickly took us all in—Dad, me, Buzzy.

"What are you all doing here?" he asked.

"This is Ronnie's son, Scotty," she said. "He's a freshman at Baylor. You must be coaching here now."

"I am," he said. He extended his hand to me. "I'm so glad to meet you, Scotty," he said.

I shook his hand. *Almost an apparition.*

"If you ever want to know anything about your father, come and see me anytime," he said kindly. "I'd be happy to talk with you."

"Thank you," I said. I meant it.

I never went.

We spent Thanksgiving Day with Mom's older sister, Aunt Lois, in Fort Worth.

My cousins, Jim and Dede, had compiled their mother's old, 8-millimeter home movies and transferred them to videotape. There were shots of us all as preschoolers—Tommy, trying to crowd in on Jim's birthday party. Buzzy, in his cowboy gear. Me, a stick figure wearing a pointed birthday hat on an outsized head. I got some needling from the peanut gallery. "The head," Jim roared, "the head."

There was footage of Robbie, Jim and Dede's younger brother. Robbie had been closest in age to Buzzy—and closest, we'd thought, in temperament. Like Buzzy, he also was flamingly red-haired, and loud. But Robbie had grown up to be a sweet-natured, gracious teenager.

Five years after Tommy died, Robbie developed a mysterious heart ailment. His doctors thought he'd recovered fully, and they gave him permission to run in a track meet. But just after Robbie finished the race, his heart stopped. He was buried next to Tommy, in Waxahachie.

Next came a segment in black and white.

"Oh, Scotty, look here," Aunt Lois urged.

The images were blurred, the camera unsteady. Four figures materialized. They stood stiffly, looking into the camera. On the left, I realized, were Aunt Lois and Uncle James, holding Jim as an infant. Next to them stood Mom, holding Tommy, and Daddy Ronnie.

"That's your Daddy Ronnie," Aunt Lois said. "Oh, Scotty, he was such a nice guy."

I remembered hearing my Uncle James—Daddy Ronnie's fraternity brother—saying something similar. "A *great* guy, Scotty. Just a tremendous guy."

I looked closely at the flickering image. It was more than a photograph. It was *him*—actually moving.

He wasn't wearing his usual friendly smile for the camera. He looked annoyed, bothered by something.

I wanted to ask if anybody remembered why. But I didn't.

I wrote an essay in my freshman composition class about looking into a mirror, wondering who I was. I referred to Ronnie— a subject, I realized, I'd never fully examined. I'd wanted to write of how I'd grown inescapably into his shoes. Yet, as I tried to put the words on paper, I realized I had no idea what I was trying to say. The essay ran here and there, all over the place, full of delayed adolescent angst and overarching melancholy. But I knew how I wanted to end it, and I did so on a melodramatic note: "I am my father's son."

I didn't send the essay to Mom, as I might have done. Instead, I sent it to Cleta. As usual, my godmother responded warmly, yet with judicious words: "Yes, you are your father's son. But you are even more so your *heavenly* Father's son."

They weren't the words I'd wanted to read.

Ghosts

The next summer, Buzzy and I drove to Brady to visit Tody. Back through the changing landscape, into the mesa-dotted country. Back through time.

It was our first trip together as a duo. Buzzy had just finished his freshman year in high school and had reached an athletic six feet. Now we could genuinely compete against each other in individual sports.

We hadn't seen our grandmother in years. Tody lived in town now. She'd had to sell the farm after Grandjesse died. Her house was a white-frame cottage with a well-kept yard and garden. Inside, it smelled the way the farmhouse had. This was partly because she'd made all the desserts we'd liked as kids—strawberry cake, banana pudding with homemade vanilla filling, pineapple upside-down cake.

On Saturday morning, Tody's three sisters came for a visit—Aunt Babe, whom we knew, and Aunt Vide and Aunt Opal, whom we'd never met. They arrived early. When Buzzy and I finally roused ourselves and went to the living room, Tody and her sisters were sitting in chairs, all in a row. Buzzy and I plunked ourselves on the couch.

Tody, the oldest, was the quiet soul of the four. Aunt Vide—decked out in lengthy shorts, swirling-cone hair, and dangling earrings—was the energy and humor. She spun into a story about a nephew of hers who'd become an early success.

"Now, *he* was ambitious."

Buzzy yawned without apology.

I listened, rapt. For what I wasn't sure. Our conversation was the expected, chatty catch-up on family illnesses, our parents' work, our subjects in school. But I didn't pay too much attention to the words. It was the faces, the voices I tried to soak up—the tones, the gestures, miles of distance I wanted to shorten.

My brother and I lugged our tennis racquets to an outdoor court that afternoon. The Brady sun beat down on us hotter than usual, but we were determined to last an entire match.

Buzzy couldn't get over Vide. "Man, she is hilarious," he said.

Maybe the sun was a little too hot. We ended up arguing, over nothing probably, but we both were resolute, stubborn. We walked back to Tody's house separately. Buzzy steamed, I trembled.

On the drive home, we stopped in Blanket to see Aunt Louise and Uncle Pinky. Our aunt greeted us in the driveway as she always had: "Hi, sweet boys."

After lunch, Uncle Pinky drove us out to the pasture in his pickup, for old times' sake. As we passed a wooded area, a few wild turkeys scattered from the brush. "There goes Tom Turkey, heading for the hills," our uncle quipped. Buzzy laughed.

We stopped at a livestock tank, so Uncle Pinky could check on the water level. As we climbed out, some turtles peeked their heads just above the surface.

"Time for a little target practice, ya think?" Uncle Pinky said. He reached inside the truck's cab and pulled out his .22 rifle.

He fired into the water. One turtle ducked. Another surfaced. After a few shots, our uncle had come within an inch or two of his targets.

He held out the rifle to me with a grin. "Here, have a try," he said.

"Oh, no," I said. "That's okay."

"You sure?"

"Yes, sir."

He turned to Buzzy. "How 'bout it, Buzzer?"

"Sure," Buzzy said. He took the rifle and rested it on his shoulder. He fired once, missing a turtle's head by about a foot.

Buzz laughed at himself. "Mind if I try again?" he asked.

"Not at all, go ahead."

He took a couple more shots. He came closer to the turtles each time, carefully adjusting his aim to how far he'd missed on the previous shot.

"There you go," Uncle Pinky said.

After a half-dozen shots, Buzzy also had come within a few inches. Then he handed the rifle back to our uncle.

"Through?" Uncle Pinky said.

"Yeah, I'm not gonna get any closer," Buzzy answered.

"You sure?"

"Yes, sir."

Aunt Louise loaded us down with food for the drive home. Up the highway a few miles, we stopped at a service station for some drinks, and we ate in the car as I drove. After we'd finished, Buzzy napped in the passenger seat.

Why couldn't I be as casual about things as he was? I thought.

17

I was at home in Waxahachie one weekend when a heavy windstorm hit. The gales were so fierce, they split our big front yard tree in two. The next morning, all the footballs Tommy and Buzzy had lost in the tree's branches lay spat onto the ground.

I held up an old, scarred NFL Duke—Tommy's prize possession. "Wow," I marveled. "I never thought we'd see this again." I tossed it to Buzz.

"Hey," he grinned, "you think it's got any life left?"

Buzzy and I had never been in high school at the same time. When I was a senior, he was in eighth grade. And while I was away at Baylor for four years, Buzzy had been at Waxahachie, excelling in several things, particularly sports. When he graduated, Texas A&M gave him a scholarship for his punting ability.

"I didn't know they gave scholarships to punters," I told him.

"You do now," he said.

I was at home the day Buzzy left for College Station. He and I were talking in the back bedroom—Tommy's and my old room, now his—when Dad walked in. He'd come to say goodbye. Buzzy turned to face him, his back toward me. Dad hugged him, his face visible to me over Buzzy's shoulder. I saw my father's eyes crinkle for the first time. His lips bloated, as if they were about to burst.

It scared me. I looked away. Gingerly, I stepped into the next room.

I stood there for another minute or so, waiting for them to part.

So that's what he looked like, I thought.

Buzzy's body had filled out to be like Dad's, only on a larger scale. He'd played tight end at Waxahachie, as well as handling all duties related to kicking. After his first visit home from A&M,

he was even bigger. He also was eager to demonstrate his physical superiority to me.

I was in graduate school in Virginia at the time. Whenever I came home for holidays, he and I spent most of our time engaged in some kind of innocuous competition. A favorite was full-body-contact Nerf basketball. We shut all four doors to the central hallway of the house, sealing ourselves into the small, five-by-eight-foot space. Then we hung a plastic hoop at either end. The point was to get past your opponent by whatever means necessary to score. Of course, you had nowhere to go but *through* him. So the space became a cage, a hothouse, Mad Max's Thunderdome. Buzzy once shoulder-slammed me so hard, I went through a bathroom door, knocking it off the hinges.

I had no idea my brother was using his brawn for anything more than a competitive advantage. After one contest, he admitted, "I couldn't wait till I got to be this age. That's all I could think about when I was little—how I was going to really *give it* to you and Tommy."

Here I was, having to absorb his wrath alone. Where was Tommy now, when I needed him?

Nor was Buzzy afraid to name our other transgressions. "You probably don't remember half the things you guys told me," he said.

Such as?

"Like when I went to get my first physical for peewee football. You said the doctors would give me a shot in the stomach with a square needle."

I grinned.

"Then you said they were going to put my head in a vise, to see how much pressure I could take."

I winced.

We relished pointing out our differences to each other and laughing about them. One was my curiosity about all things religious.

"Do you remember telling me about Peter Marshall?" Buzzy said.

Who?

"The preacher."

That Peter Marshall. I had no idea why I would ever tell Buzzy anything about the Reverend Peter Marshall. The only thing I knew about him was from watching a movie Mom had recommended when I was a kid. It starred Richard Todd. And it oddly combined the episodic qualities of fifties biopics with the choral sentiments of religious costume dramas. All I remembered about it was the conversion scene. Marshall was still a young man at the time, wandering blindly through a fog in the woods. Just as he was about to step over the edge of a cliff, he tripped on a log. It saved his life.

"That guy," Buzzy continued. "You're telling me about this preacher who's traveling around the world for God. And I'm confused, because all this time I think you're talking about the host of 'Hollywood Squares.'"

Mom and I were prone to talk about such things at length. Whereas, if a spiritual subject didn't interest Buzz, he had no trouble getting up and leaving the room.

"Do you know what Mom told me about you one time?" He gleefully affected a mystical tone: "'Buzz, Scotty's a romantic dreamer.'" He howled at this, couldn't stop laughing. The *ridiculousness* of the thought.

My brother didn't know that I cried at his college football games. This always took me by surprise. I didn't get to attend many games, because I lived in Virginia. The first time I saw Buzzy play in person was at College Station. I had met up with an old undergraduate friend in Dallas, and my parents drove us to the game. Seventy thousand people crammed into Kyle Field, a good portion Aggie corpsmen, yelling in unison the entire time. Fourth down comes, and out trots my little brother, casually, wearing maroon. I have no idea why I felt so overwhelmed. I kept up the banter with my Baylor buddy—typical, cynical-young-man sports talk—but I had to turn away to hide my tears.

As it turned out, the head coach at A&M who had recruited Buzzy was fired after my brother's freshman year. When the new coach came in, he cleaned house. He didn't think twice about revoking scholarships from the players the previous coach had brought in. Buzzy was one of them.

Buzz didn't allow himself to get shaken up over it. As soon as Dad got the news, he contacted the head coach at Baylor, and landed Buzzy a chance to walk on. Buzz enrolled but had to sit out football the following year. When he finally got to play, he earned a scholarship. Twelve years later, when the century-old Southwest Conference dissolved, Buzzy held the conference record for single-game punting average.

I hadn't responded so positively to the A&M massacre. I was outraged not only that a coach could do this to a player, but that he could get away with it so cleanly. I wrote to John Underwood, a writer for *Sports Illustrated*, who'd authored a book on corruption in college athletics. He responded sympathetically but acknowledged that Buzzy had had no recourse.

As I looked back on it later, I remembered how shaken I'd been. When I reread the letter I'd written to Underwood, I was embarrassed by it. The rage in it scared me. Even after the ordeal turned out to be a hidden blessing, I hadn't been able to shake my anger at the coach.

"You and Mom talk about that as if it were some kind of terrible thing I had to go through," Buzzy said. "It wasn't like that. I just had to move on. Life's too short."

I had only been aware of our differences. Then I got a call from another old college friend, Tom Day, who had stayed at Baylor to go to grad school.

"Tell me, Scotty," he said, "is Buzzy Sawyer, the Baylor punter, your *brother* Buzzy?"

"The very one."

"I *knew* it," he said. "All this time I thought he was still an Aggie. Well, I'm hanging around campus last Thanksgiving, and I go to the stadium to watch the Texas game. It's fourth down, and they announce *Buzzy Sawyer*. I look up and see those bowed-back Sawyer legs. I knew he had to be related."

I never knew that I had Sawyer legs. Or that Buzzy and I shared the same type of legs. In that respect—the *bowed-back* aspect—we did. We each have our mother's legs.

18

A movie in old newsreel style. Woody Allen is a chameleon-like character early in the century. He turns up in the midst of virtually every historic event, glad-handing with famous people of the time. He identifies himself so completely with whomever he's around, he actually takes on that person's physical characteristics—from a circus fat man, to a bearded rabbi, to the U.S. President.

The media exposes him as a psychological phenomenon—a person completely vacuous of any personal identity. He's taken to an isolated house in the woods to be studied by a famous psychologist, played by Mia Farrow. She subjects him to daily sessions of hypnosis to try to unearth the true self beneath this "cypher."

For days he continues to be completely subservient, though, his every interaction aimed to please the psychologist. Finally, there's a break-through. Under hypnosis, he complains about the pancakes the psychologist cooks for him each morning.

Over time, his true self begins to emerge more fully. The psychologist takes him on outings to events, gatherings, galleries, constantly asking for his opinion on things. He responds timidly at first, then more assertively as the days pass. Ultimately, his tastes are revealed to be hopelessly middlebrow.

The smog in Los Angeles is worst in summers. That's when the air is relatively dead, so the smog drifts slowly inland, nudged by the ocean breezes, hazy pink-brown clouds pushing up against the San Gabriel Mountains. They stop dead there and linger all afternoon, in the foothills. It makes for great sunsets. But if you live in a foothills town, as I did during my first professional job—in the tiny village of Sierra Madre, nestled between Pasadena and Arcadia—you come home after work and look out over the L.A. Basin to see . . . nothing. Every once in a while you get a decent Santa Ana wind blowing in over the San Gabriels that clears everything off. But that's a rare day. More often, there's a fine haze clouding everything.

People told me it would take a couple of years to get used to the seasons in southern California. After I'd been there for two years, I did notice, one odd January afternoon, that the temperature hadn't risen above fifty. If you're not careful, they said, you can end up drifting from one season to another, without knowing it. Soon all the seasons run together, and you don't know a beginning from an end. Such is life, I was told, for an Angeleno.

I didn't have much trouble adapting to my first job. I had joined the staff of a small magazine as its associate editor. At its core, I thought, editing is a simple task. All you have to do is adapt yourself to the writer's voice—to immerse yourself in it, until you're absorbed by its rhythms, its patterns, its functions—and go with the flow. Line after line, your job is to preserve order—to reign in chaos, put things into place, make seemingly meaningless things make sense. In the end, it's a matter of making every line count. You're a guardian of the lines.

In my second job, I was responsible for producing a monthly magazine. This was a quantum step up in responsibility. During the first few months of my watch, however, some loose end was always falling off around deadline time. I had to start keeping a daily organizer—listing things, categorizing, prioritizing. I couldn't afford to overlook anything.

At night, I went to a lot of movies, often by myself. The art houses and retrospective theaters around Pasadena—the Esquire, the Colorado, the Rialto—showed the kind of features that faithfully transported you beyond the norm. I saw a lot of good new films—Gregory Nava's *El Norte,* Jim Jarmusch's *Stranger Than Paradise,* Wim Wenders' *Paris, Texas*—and also caught up on the canonical works, with double features of classics at the Rialto: *Jules and Jim* paired with *The 400 Blows; The Maltese Falcon* with *The Glass Key; The Bicycle Thief* with *Open City.* After I'd seen enough art films and classics, Hollywood's contemporary output began to look formulaic and predictable.

The one thing that drove me nuts about mainstream movies more than anything was how they treated death. In most cases, a character's death came as a matter of convenience—say, a cad was killed, so his saintly wife could remarry. Or a villain was killed by someone other than the hero, so the hero didn't have to taint himself by killing. In these cases, death lost its price and pain. Instead, it was all about the viewer's relief. Cheap relief. Death is *always* about more than that, I thought, no matter whose it is.

One evening I invited a few friends from the magazine over to screen a couple of videos—*His Girl Friday,* the rapid-fire, wise-cracking Howard Hawks newspaper classic, and Stanley Donen's romantic *Two For The Road,* with Albert Finney and Audrey Hepburn. I'd seen both movies already. After we'd finished dinner, it was too late to watch both, so we opted for Donen.

I'd remembered *Two For The Road* as a bittersweet, insightful look at a marriage. More bitter than sweet, as it turned out. Breakups. Adultery. Bitter confrontations. My friends' expressions said it all afterward, as they filed grimly out the door.

I tried to cook for myself in my apartment once a week. The meals weren't complicated—usually a steak, baked potato, vegetable—but with every meal, I concerned myself that each element came out finished at the same time. Once, while I was browning some meat on the stove, I realized I was missing some ingredients. I lived only two blocks from the small corner grocery store. I convinced myself I could leave the meat cooking, get to the store quickly, and be back in a few minutes, so I wouldn't have to stop everything in the middle of the process. It would require perfect timing—just the kind of inconsequential little risk I relished.

I hurried to the store to pick up the extra things I needed. By the time I found everything, though, the checkout lines had grown atypically long. I quickly had to count the cost of either waiting in line or dropping everything and hurrying home. What if the meat on the stove cooked through, started smoking, then flaming, then caught the apartment on fire? What if my neighbors paid for my seemingly inconsequential task with their lives?

I decided to hold my ground. The shoppers ahead of me in line moved slowly, agonizingly so. As soon as I was handed my change, I shot into a dead sprint, clutching my plastic grocery bag. Everybody I passed seemed to move in slow motion—a patron exiting the corner bar, a neighbor watering his lawn, a woman jogging. When I got home, I burst open the door, puffing.

Everything was fine. Another small yet dangerous task accomplished. The dinner came out perfectly.

A day later my car was stolen. I was aghast. This kind of stuff didn't happen in tiny Sierra Madre.

I had to report it missing to the police. My insurance company provided me with a car, and when I arrived late at the office, everybody asked why I'd pulled up in a hideous orange compact.

"My car got stolen," I explained.

"Give the police two days," my boss said. "They'll find it in East L.A. Once you get down there, they'll hand you the steering wheel, a spark plug, and your key chain."

Two days later, the police did call. They'd found my car.

"Mr. Sawyer, could you meet us at the corner of Sierra Madre Boulevard and Arcadia Drive? You'll see us in the parking lot."

The thieves had ditched it in my own town—and just a few blocks from my house, no less. I could walk to the corner they mentioned.

As I made the trek, I wondered where the car had been all that time—if whoever stole it had kept it hidden somewhere in town.

A half block away, I saw the two officers hovering around my car, peering through the windows to the interior.

Then it dawned on me—I'd driven my car to the store three days ago. When I was cooking dinner. *And left it there.*

"Mr. Sawyer," one of the policemen said soberly, "would you please check the vehicle to see if anything's missing."

I stared at him, unable to speak.

"We need to find out if anything has been taken," he reiterated.

"Officer," I said, "I'm sorry."

The policemen glanced at each other.

"I realized something on the way over here," I said. "I parked my car here three days ago, and, ah—I forgot about it."

The officers looked across the street to the corner bar. They grinned knowingly and shook their heads.

"Don't worry about it," one of them said. "Happens all the time."

One year I decided to spend Christmas in L.A. instead of going home. I wanted to do it just to see what it was like being some-where else on Christmas Day. Mom and Dad didn't protest, but I sensed their disappointment. I was resolute, however. I vol-unteered at the L.A. Rescue Mission, and a couple of actors showed up and dished out food with us.

I'd thought I might feel something, anything, while doing this, but I didn't. Of course, I knew better—that doing good works wouldn't provide the warm feeling you might be seeking from God. But that wasn't what I was after. I just hadn't known what else to do with myself. When I left the mission that after-noon, I had no idea how to fill the day.

I sat up late, watching *A Christmas Memory* with Geraldine Page. It was followed by *It's a Wonderful Life,* the Frank Capra classic. At the end, Jimmy Stewart, surrounded by his friends and family, realized that no matter how bad things got, life truly was a gift.

I switched off the TV when the credits finished rolling. Then I lay on the sofa until I fell asleep.

The next time I flew home, Buzzy met me at the gate. I'd arrived on a large plane, and it was a full flight. I was among the final people walking through the gate.

When I saw Buzz, he grinned at me accusingly.

"I'll bet your seat was at the front of the plane," he said as we shook hands.

It was.

"And I'll bet you let everybody get off before you, didn't you?"

I did.

Every so often, when I signed a check for something, a clerk commented on my name.

"Sawyer, huh? Got a brother named Tom?"

Yeah, whatever.

I was having a hard time keeping up with the simple requirements of the magazine. I'd never liked making phone calls—asking people to make deadlines, rewrite articles, accept an assignment. Now I wasn't simply leaving that task for last; I put it off indefinitely. Every few months, a weekday came when I lay in bed knowing I couldn't face work. I called in sick. Sociologists say this isn't unusual in high-stress workplaces, and at times mine was one. But I knew better.

My mistakes at work were draining me of something vital, some central reservoir. Some mornings I apologized to God before going in. At first my prayers were to be able to keep a

clear head throughout the day, so I wouldn't overlook something. After a while, they centered on something else—my compulsion to please the people around me. The more mistakes I
made, the more eager I was to appease someone, even when I
knew that what I was offering to do was wrong. I assured my
boss that an article would be written by a certain time, when I
knew it wouldn't be. Or, I assured my writers that my boss
would like their articles, when I knew he wouldn't.

It became harder and harder to open the Bible. I saw myself in
every judgment-worthy character: the wayward nation in Jere-
miah. The self-justifying Pharisee in Matthew. The guileful
magician, Simon, in Acts. No matter what church I attended, I
felt the same sort of heavy cloud over my soul.

I decided to spend an entire Saturday praying atop the hill
at Griffith Observatory. The site overlooks the whole L.A.
Basin. I'd wanted to have a full day to make myself available.
But I got a late start—dallying till after lunch, revising my to-do
list, ticking off my tasks angrily. During the drive there, I convinced myself I'd already ruined my mission.

I sat in one spot, under a tree, the whole afternoon. I was
determined to hear from God. To hear a voice that, now that I
was on my own, I wondered if I'd ever heard for myself.

Late that afternoon, I stood and brushed the grass from my
pants. L.A. still looked the same.

six

Resurrections

What? Shall we receive good at the hand of God,
and shall we not receive evil?

—Job 2:10

19

Tom Cruise is Ron Kovic, a young Vietnam vet who lost the use of his legs in battle. Now he's back home, in a veteran's hospital. He's determined to be rehabilitated. After several agonizing months of rehab, Ron tries to walk on crutches—but he trips, falls, and reinjures himself. His injury becomes permanent.

Ron tries to adjust to life back home, but he finds more pain at every turn. His old friends take him to bars, where he tries to dance by doing wheelies in his chair. The women he meets only see him as a novelty.

One night he comes home drunk. He begins to lash out—at his parents and siblings, at the war, at God.

Finally, his distraught father lifts him from his chair and helps him to bed. "What is it you want, Ronnie?" he asks.

Ron begins sobbing.

"I want to be a man again."

His father shakes his head, helpless.

"Who's gonna love me, Dad?" Ron finally asks. "Who's gonna love me now?"

Buzzy had to leave the theater during the rehab scenes. We were there with our wives. Joy and I had come to Houston to visit Buzz and his wife, Cristal, in their new home. All of us had been married only a couple of years.

I lost control several times during the movie. When it ended and we were walking out, I ducked into the men's room. I closed the door to a stall and leaned against it, my face in my hands for ten minutes.

When I came out, Buzzy was standing alone in the lobby. Joy and Cristal were outside in the sunlight, their arms crossed, their faces drawn, talking and nodding.

I had to ask my brother.

"Why'd you leave?"

He shook his head. "I just couldn't take it."

"Take what?"

"Those hospital scenes."

"What about them?"

He shrugged. "I don't know. I just couldn't take it."

Joy and I live in an area of Denver most people call "downtown." It's actually a half mile from downtown proper, where the office buildings begin to rise. Our house is an old, two-story "Denver square." As you look out our living room window, you gaze down the walk between two tall blue spruces, beyond the silver maples lining our block, and across the street to our neighbors' houses, a variety of prewar brick duplexes and other Denver squares. A few years ago, Joy planted two hundred tulip and daffodil bulbs in alternating rows along our sidewalk. Except for the mornings when elementary-age schoolboys walk by and absent-mindedly tear off a flower head or two, the front bed is thriving.

Resurrections

I have a mindless routine I rehearse whenever Joy leaves for a rare trip by herself. The night before she goes, as she's packing, I start a long list of things to do that weekend. I take loose-leaf sheets from my organizer and start penciling in tasks that fill every hour. When I've finished and I sit back to look at what I plan to do, my head gets woozy. I've filled every moment with something—even if it's some mindless activity like going to a movie or watching a game on TV. Once I realize I've overloaded, I erase and start over. I make adjustments to allow myself some breathing room. But even then, the days end up packed.

As I drive Joy to the airport, I'm already antsy. When I peck her goodbye, I'm thinking about the first item on the list. The list, the list, the list.

Once she's gone, however, I never get started. By the afternoon, I've ended up on the sofa—mindlessly channel-flipping, berating myself for getting started so late and then scratching the whole works. Hating myself for doing nothing. Hating that nothing seems worth doing.

We met in Virginia, where I edited a newsletter for a nonprofit religious organization. She was a senior writer in the office two doors down. We got to know each other late in the afternoons, when we had long, involved dialogues, mostly on writing. We started exchanging books from our shelves—my novels and books on writing, her books on poetry, counseling, and practical theology.

We both played basketball in the company's intramural league. She'd played college ball at a small, Midwestern liberal arts college, a Christian school. We started driving to and from the intramural games together. Soon we were trading stories about our hometown experiences in Waxahachie and Colby, Kansas. Talking was easy. And she could laugh. In fact, she could do both interchangeably, whether the conversation was light or deep.

So I began telling her things. About my faith, my brothers, my parents, my God. My sins. The dark novels I gravitated to. The harsh movies I sought out.

She told me things too.

My coworkers arched their eyebrows when they learned about our first date. I'd asked Joy to accompany me to a speech by Elie Wiesel, the Holocaust survivor.

"Ever heard of dinner and a movie?" someone suggested.

I'd read *Night,* Wiesel's short, harrowing novel based on his experiences at Auschwitz. But I was drawn to him mostly by something I'd read in an interview with him. He said that when he emerged from the camps, where each member of his family had died, he vowed not to speak of the experience for ten years.

Joy didn't complain throughout the sober, brainy evening. In exchange for her good faith, and for lasting through it all, I stopped spontaneously at a convenience store on the way home. I came out a helium-filled balloon, a cellophane-wrapped rose, and a pink plastic broach in the shape of sunglasses.

"You can't say I never gave you anything," I said.

We did movies. The whole gamut.

Therese. Bare-bones life of the saint, in French.

Amazon Women on the Moon. Unsaintly laughs, in fifties sci-fi.

And poetry. The everyday kind.

Comic twists of song lyrics, exchanged in late-night deliriums as we cruised Atlantic Avenue. Pop songs, commercials, mundane metronomics—all turned on their heads by the call-and-response of poet and editor, of one glass brimming and one half-empty, she a playful McCartney to my cynical Lennon.

Words.

    Not to be ordered and arranged, but pulled out of the air. Not to be perfected, but blurted.

    Our *words.*

    Juxtaposition of left and right brain spheres. Common ground of hearts.

One day at the office, she handed me a file folder. It was an inch thick with paper.

    "What's this?"

    "Some poetry," she said.

    I sat up that night reading her life's work in one hundred and fifty pages.

    The range of subjects was astonishing. Yet it was the voice that floored me—sober truths, learned before their time. Yet all expressed in clear-eyed love. The voice of one who'd seen a lot.

    "Hey," I asked the next day, "when did you write these?"

    Between the ages of eight and eighteen.

    I held up one particular poem. It voiced the grief of an entire community.

    "What about this one?" I said. "How old were you when you wrote it?"

    "Fourteen."

    I looked into her face, her eyes. I thought of things no words could explain. I reached across her desk and stroked her cheek, brushed back her hair.

Dark hair, dark eyes. Ruby lips.

    Yvonne DeCarlo?

    Yikes!

A poet.

    Not of simple rhymes, but of rhythms. The big rhythms.

I struck out for a matinee once, on a rare day when we weren't together. The Naro, a retrospective house Joy and I frequented, was screening an old favorite of mine, *The Year of Living Dangerously*. Mel Gibson and Sigourney Weaver. It was everything I'd remembered it to be. Moody atmosphere, sensitive direction, human passion, spiritual compassion—all the things that had compelled me about it before.

Yet as I sat absorbing it again, it looked different. *Felt* different. The harshness of the Indonesian world it depicted, harsher. The attraction between Mel and Sigourney, deeper. And the words, resounding, as I'd never heard them. Words, even, from the gospel of Luke, spoken by the Billy Kwan character, shedding a glaring light on the suffering world it addressed.

The movie was ... *more*.

And yet somehow, refreshingly, less.

As usual, the sun blinded me when I walked out of the theater. It felt good to be outside.

How do you know when you're in love?

I wanted to be with her when she was old.

I couldn't stand to think about the years passing between us, without my being near her. I wanted to see her when the raven hair turned to snow. I wanted every small mile-marker. Every ripe day, and every still one. Every line of poetry written in a casual conversation. Every touch, every kiss deepened by—

By what, exactly?

Familiarity? Permanence?

What on this earth is permanent?

What can remain familiar, if it's impermanent?

Deepened by—

Resurrections

I didn't know. Who can ever know that?

Love. Faith.
 Inseparable.

20

During our first year of marriage, we lived in New York. We'd had a friend over for dinner and were enjoying coffee in our living room. When the conversation turned to our families, I opened my wallet to show our friend some pictures of my family. We continued chatting as he flipped through the photos. Suddenly, he froze.

"Who's this?" he asked. He held out the wallet.

It was Daddy Ronnie.

"That's my first father," I said.

"Not the one you've been talking about?"

"No. That's my second father. He married Mom after my first father died."

Our friend gazed down at the photo. He looked up again, searching my face.

"The resemblance is incredible."

I'd written a letter to Aunt Louise, Daddy Ronnie's sister, when Joy and I were still living in New York. I was responding to a letter she'd written earlier, maybe even a year or two before. I'd often let that happen with letters. Now my aunt wrote me back, saying she'd finally been going through some of Tody's things after she died. She was gathering a few mementos of Daddy Ronnie's to send me.

A few months later, I received a box from Blanket. I set the box on a bookshelf next to my side of the bed, alongside the books and magazines I read at night.

"What did Aunt Louise send you?" Joy asked.

"I don't know," I said. "Haven't opened it up just yet."

A year later, the box moved with us to Denver. It was still unopened. I laid it on the floor beside a small writing desk in our bedroom, where I kept important things.

Another year passed. One Saturday morning, Joy left to run some errands that would occupy her most of the day. I was still in bed when she left. I rolled over and saw the box. I decided to lie in bed a while longer.

When I got up, I took out the trash. I vacuumed. I unloaded, loaded, and started the dishwasher. I straightened out my half of the closet. I poked through the office in our spare bedroom, looking to find some extra work I might finish, but there was none.

I had never dreamed about my first father. So I never had to wake up to the same sad realization whenever I dreamed about Tommy: *he was here—I saw him, I felt him, he was truly real. But I know he's dead now. And when I wake up, I'm going to feel it all over again.*

I couldn't be grateful for the dreams that never came about Daddy Ronnie. I couldn't feel the thrilling reminder that he had been alive with me at one time, and that he was alive someplace right now—and I'd been allowed to feel that, if only in my sleep.

I never knew to *want* to dream about him.

It was just a box, I told myself. An unopened brown box. With my aunt's return address, "Blanket, Texas." With things inside.

The first photo was of my father as an infant. Aunt Louise was in the frame, sitting nearby. His adolescent sister—beaming with pride at her baby brother crawling around on the floor. She'd written a caption at the time of the photo, in a schoolgirl's handwriting and language.

I thumbed slowly through the other photos. There was one of him as a young boy, kneeling and holding his pet rabbit. One of him as an adolescent, standing in front of an old gymnasium, wearing an ill-fitting football uniform. One as a crew-cut, teenage hurdler. One as a ten-year-old, standing next to Uncle Pinky. There was also a letter Uncle Pinky had written to him from the Pacific during World War II. It was jovial, patriotic, brotherly.

My father.

I saw his hair grow from loose to wiry. I saw his face grow from round and cherubic in childhood, to big-eared and long-nosed in adolescence, to triangular and sharp-featured in high school. I saw his frame grow from soft and kidlike, to long and gangly, to tall and taut.

His life unfolded before me in black and white. And slowly, as I let the reality behind the images sink in, I saw Daddy Ronnie in a way I hadn't before—in a way our family's anguished prison hadn't allowed. I saw *a man*—no longer a ghost in our house, the *other* father whose pictures were still around. I saw him now in relation to others—as other people's brother, son, nephew, friend.

It built slowly in me as I made my way through the box. His whiskers were bristly under my fingers. I smelled his sweat. I saw dust flying off his pants. Then, oh then, yes—I felt the warmth of my father's hand. I felt the pride in it, as he reached to me across decades of strife, pain, and hidden grief, and he shook mine with pride. Oh, Lord, how had I missed him? He's real, a real man, *my father*—somewhere still living—someone who would tell me I'm a man, but never could.

I lost my composure at every new revelation. As I pored over the photos, my fingers wet, his image became ever clearer. A baby, a boy, a teenager, a man. I wondered how he must have felt at each stage of life. There were so many simple pleasures in the photos. So many things ahead of him.

What would he have been like had he lived? What would we all have been like?

I wanted to ask him—so, what do you think about Joy? Did you ever like any of the girls I brought home? I liked the num-

ber eight when I was little, and I've never been able to explain
it. Can you tell me? What was Mom like before you died? Was
she melancholy then, or just a handful for you?

Were you able to be sad when Tommy died? Would you
have cried at his funeral? When he was suffering, did you see
your own body withering away in his?

Then, as quickly as the feeling had come, it began to fade.
The connection was being lost. This happened in all my tender moments with Joy, whenever I broke and wept and connected with her. I could stay in it, maintain it, for maybe half an
hour, a precious half an hour. Then, back to jokes. Back to my
lists. Now, like a morphing film image, my father's tan skin was
rapidly turning grainy and gray. His round, sweating forehead
flattened into paper.

Don't go.

I didn't know how to act for a while after that—how to move or
feel, how to think. I'd seen something, discovered a living person—someone who could tell me something about myself that
no one else could—and now I couldn't go back. Nor did I want
to. It was as if I'd witnessed some vision that no one else had
seen.

I had to remind myself that, oh yes, others had seen the
image I'd seen. That my mother had known him in full—had
shared a beginning with him, a young dream, and two children.
That maybe Tommy had known him after all—touched and
tasted him, for just long enough.

Daddy Ronnie had been *ours.*

Yet, I'd never been able to look at him. To gaze into him—
through Mom, through Tommy, even through my own *eight
weeks with him.* I'd always had to move my eyes away quickly.

Guilt.

Why?

21

Tues., Oct. 11, 1994
Dear Scotty (and always to Joy, too!),
It was such a deep thrill to read your letter—I can understand your feelings and tears as you have discovered for the first time pieces and degrees of development about your father. That is the reason I wanted you to have all those pictures. I have many pictures and so do our children. Charles adored Ronnie. He was 12 when Ronnie passed away, leaving a gap in his young, sensitive life (until his own Ronnie Charles was born 16 years ago). We have our memories, Scotty, and that's what I'd like to share with you, but I'll do that separately and a little later.
Keep in touch—we love you,
Aunt Louise
(and Uncle Pinky)
I would have shared many years sooner, but we love Robert, and I wouldn't do anything that might make him feel any less of a father to you.

I was talking with an older woman in our church. She'd been a missionary for years, had seen a lot, and was always warm and encouraging. She listened intently during conversations and thought deeply about others' words.

She asked about my family, and I briefly summed up our history—my first father's death, my mother's remarriage, my growing appreciation for my second father.

"So," she reflected after a few minutes of conversation, "you know what it feels like to be an adopted child of the Father."

I thought about that.

"I'm not sure what you mean," I said.

What is a stepfather? Does it mean *a step removed?* Is the word *step* supposed to mark some formal boundary—an arm's length that keeps your second father from being what he is in reality, *your father?*

Then I didn't know what a stepfather was. It certainly didn't describe Dad.

What is a natural father? I didn't know that, either, I thought.

Did I?

Stu Lumpkins is my other best friend from Waxahachie—the third member of a fraternal trio with Big John and me. Like John, Stu had become a lawyer. A few years ago, he came to Denver on business, and he stayed at our house rather than at a hotel. After dinner, coffee, and a full evening of laughter and catching up, Joy knowingly excused herself, to allow me to talk with my old buddy into the wee hours.

Six years before, Stu had been treated for cancer. He and his wife, Theresa, had adopted two beautiful girls, the second at the very height of Stu's chemotherapy treatments. In fact, as Stu sat at one end of the hospital, a bag of poison dripping into his arm, his younger adoptive daughter was about to be delivered at the other end. Stu received his deadly treatment on Good Friday. Nicole was born on Easter Sunday.

Now my friend had been given a clean bill of health. He and Theresa even looked forward to possibly adopting a third child. We had a lot to celebrate that night. And we were doing just that—reliving and recounting the incredible gifts we'd each received—when the conversation turned to Stu's girls. He told me his oldest, Hannah, age five, had shown a prodigious talent for the stage.

"She knows her way around a mike," Stu said. "She'll ask a question, then point the mike at the other kid and wait for his response."

"Where'd she get that?"

"I don't know. Maybe she's paying attention when we flip by some talk show. She just knows what's supposed to be happening on the stage at all times. I took our camcorder to tape their kindergarten show. I was looking through the lens, trying to find her in the kids' chorus. When I spotted her, she was motioning camera directions to me."

I grinned. "Ever wonder where that comes from?"

"Yeah." He paused. "You do wonder about it."

I wondered aloud if he would be ready for the day when Hannah and Nicole began to wonder about it.

He flinched.

"No," he said. "I can't imagine it."

We let a moment pass.

"You do think about it, though," Stu said. "The whole nature-versus-nurture thing. It's hard."

Dad had known about the box. He'd known that I'd become interested.

I tried not to think about how it must have made him feel. Here he was, I thought, at an age when he wants to reap the fruits of having been a faithful father through the years. Who wouldn't?

Now this—all this stuff you're digging up. He had no idea you'd be going through this, thirty years later.

I remembered a letter—I couldn't find it. Dad had written it to me after he knew I was investigating Ronnie. The letter was short and ostensibly about some other subject. But it contained one sentence that I feared was the whole reason he'd written:

I'm still your father.

Angry. Maybe hurt.

Afraid?

Didn't he know I'd never compared them? Didn't he know how hard I'd tried not to? And when I did, I always made *him* superior in my mind?

Did he know what it had cost me? What the high price of loyalty had exacted from the part of my soul Ronnie comprised? What I'd had to hide not just from him, but from myself?

I'm not Ronnie.

It dawned on me I'd never yelled at Dad—never in my life. Frankly, it had never crossed my mind. If it had, I'd have known I'd get my butt kicked.

That wasn't it.

This was it. *I could have lost him.*

I called home to tell my parents that Joy and I were planning a trip to Blanket, to visit Aunt Louise and Uncle Pinky. Dad answered. He was friendly. Without hesitation, he recalled a trip we'd all taken to Brady, before Grandjesse died.

"We took Clyde with us," he reminded me. "Can you believe we were that stupid? They'd just had their house carpeted, and there's our filthy poodle running around all over it. We ended up staying with them for about a week. Imagine it, Scotty—that dog prancing around their house, making himself at home." He chuckled with embarrassment. "They never said a word."

I remembered the turn onto the gravel road. And their house, sitting a half mile or so back from the highway. It had been seven years.

My uncle and aunt had never seemed to age before, but now I noticed the years. Aunt Louise looked more like Tody—her face rounder than I'd remembered it. For the first time, I also saw Tommy's face in it.

"Hello, sweet boy," she said.

"Oh, you don't know how thrilled she is," Uncle Pinky said, pumping my hand.

Joy and I sat on either side of my aunt as we pored over several photograph albums. Aunt Louise slowly fingered pictures I'd never seen, photos that went back into the last century. She showed me a Methodist preacher I'd never known was in our lineage, a man of German descent. I recalled the Bible by Grandjesse's chair.

"They were from Wittenberg," she said. "That's where your father's middle name came from."

Witten. It was the name Buzzy had derived for his first daughter—Whitten.

There was a picture of young, dark-haired Grandjesse when he was courting Tody. I'd never seen a photo of him prior to his later years. He was young, slim, sly-looking.

Later that afternoon, my cousin Charles arrived with his teenage son, Ronnie. They'd driven all the way from Troy, near Killeen—almost two hours. I sat in wonder looking at the strapping kid. He had Buzzy's build, only stockier. Obviously, a weight lifter. Even his face resembled Buzzy's, I thought.

"How's Buzzy doing?" young Ronnie asked, wide-eyed.

"Great," I replied. Buzzy, the football player.

I'd waited to ask. As I looked at their beaming faces, I reconsidered. But I couldn't *not* ask them.

"Do you know why he never took the vaccine?"

Their visages sank. Now I regretted asking. But their smiles remained, as always.

"Oh, I think—" Uncle Pinky hesitated. He was trying to be fatherly—but he was searching, as I was. "You know how young people get busy," he said.

Aunt Louise heard what I was asking. She wanted to help, but couldn't.

"Oh, Scotty. I don't really know."

They'd had to tell Tody about Tommy.

"That was the hardest of all," Aunt Louise said.

I remembered Tody's tender eyes. Now I thought of all her men, whom those eyes had had to watch die. Her son. Her husband. Her grandson. Grieving at least two generations she shouldn't have had to.

The week before Joy and I were married, Aunt Louise had called to tell me that Tody had passed away. "She was in her chair, Scotty," she'd said. She'd wanted me to know my grandmother died peacefully.

A few months before Tody died, she'd gone to her lawyer to change her will. She reasoned that since both Daddy Ronnie and Tommy had died, I was next in line. So she gave me an equal share in her will, along with Aunt Louise, my father's surviving sibling. My aunt's voice had been full of joy when she shared the news with me.

No, I'd thought—the honor was all mine.

Joy and I couldn't dissuade them from treating us to a catfish dinner at a restaurant in Blanket. Uncle Pinky refused to hear our protests. He repeated, "Oh, you don't know how thrilled Louise is."

My cousin Laura and her family drove south from Dublin to meet us at the restaurant. Laura, the cousin closest in age to Tommy and me.

"How's Aunt Pat?" Laura asked. She was a teacher now herself.

"She's doing great," I said. "Getting ready to retire in a year or two. She keeps threatening, but I think it'll take a lot to part her from the kids."

Laura smiled.

Suddenly—*a flash in my brain*. What was it?

Her chin—dimpled, like Ronnie's. Her lips, spread wide, like my father's.

His smile.

It was dusk. We were driving toward a hotel in Abilene. I'd rolled the window down so we could to soak in everything—the mesas and mesquite, the sunset, the bright blue in the east.

"Scotty," Joy said softly, "when I was in the kitchen with Aunt Louise, she had this look on her face. I can't explain it to you."

Remembering.

I thought back to my aunt's expression when I asked about the polio vaccine. She had so wanted to be able to answer. Why that turn in the road took place for all of us. Why our family wasn't there through the years for our Blanket cousins' birthdays. For picnics at Brady Lake. For even a Christmas or two.

She couldn't answer. It wasn't hers to do.

I noticed the mesquite trees all leaning in the same direction—slightly eastward, bent by persistent winds.

22

The next box I received came from Mom. It had come with fair warning. When it arrived, Joy knew what it was. She brought it to the kitchen table and quietly set it before me. It contained Daddy Ronnie's letters to Mom. From the cusp of his college graduation, through Tommy's first year.

This box also sat for a while. But not quite as long.

My first father's handwriting was Tommy's. His preoccupations were mine. He reported on the minutiae of the day, as I had in college. He could be a little self-conscious, once writing an entire letter on the travails he had one morning with a lawn mower. It read as if it were intended for the humor column of some family magazine of the day.

Yet he also seemed self-aware, and good-naturedly so. He wrote to Mom, with tongue firmly in cheek, "I'm sorry you don't enjoy my weather reports."

Most impressively, to me, he knew how to let an elegiac moment speak for itself. The summer after his college gradua-tion—just before he took his first coaching job, in West—he'd gone back to Brady, to help his parents on the farm. He wrote to Mom:

We can't sleep here because of the heat, so we've been out on the porch talking and waiting for it to cool off a little. Before we had TV, that was our nightly pastime—sitting on the porch talking and watching falling stars. Sounds like something you read in a book, doesn't it?

It could have been a page torn from a Jimmy Stewart script.

But it wasn't. It was real—a real porch, with a real family sit-ting there, talking. A porch I'd sat on with my brother and my grandfather.

My father had sat in the same place where we would sit. And he'd gotten up afterward, to go inside and write a letter to our mother.

Unlike me at that age, my father seemed sure of what he wanted. In this way, his subtle force of personality was Tommy's. He might question himself before taking a first step (a trait of mine), but he moved forward resolutely. Also like Tommy: the parenthetical expressions he playfully employed in his letters—"Gasp! Choke!"— were straight out of *Mad* magazine. I remembered reading those same words aloud, alongside Tommy in the storage shed.

After graduation, he umped baseball games in Brady to make some extra money—five dollars a game. He talked with someone in town about buying a car. And he asked his parents their advice about the coaching job in West. Tody wanted him to stay in Brady, of course (he was the baby, after all—last one to leave the nest). But Grandjesse said the job in West sounded like a good opportunity. My father wrote that he suspected Grandjesse said this only so he wouldn't feel obligated to stay.

Why was he making me love him? Why now?

Why?

Why was he was making me betray Dad?

Something in me wanted Dad to stand up and call him a fake—to rip off this mask of simplicity and uprightness. To call him a sentimental mush mouth who was actually something else underneath.

Between the handwritten lines, I imagined all of Ronnie's transgressions. I began voicing them to Joy, slipping them into our conversations, one by one. Trolling for something.

Joy finally bit. "So, what is it you hate about him?" she asked calmly.

Hate about him? I don't hate anything about him.

"Then what about him bothers you? It sounds like something about him agitates you."

I don't know. He's sentimental. He makes all these little jokes. He's . . . I don't know.

"That all sounds like you."

"Heavens, yes, he was a worrier," Mom said. "He worried about debt, he worried about the future. He was very melancholy. Sometimes I might say something that set him off. He'd shut me out, to go off and figure things out for himself. He pondered things. But he'd try not to make me worry about it.

"I remember when we were dating—I went home with him to Brady for the weekend. I heard him talking with Grandjesse at the dining room table. He was asking his daddy for advice on things, and Grandjesse would answer with something like, 'Yes, son, you've got to build for the future.'"

The future.

I realized I'd rarely looked too far into it.

These letters—filling in gaps. Bridges over gaping chasms. Chasms of thirty-eight years. Chasms between his dark-featured smile in old photographs and the flesh-and-blood smiles that greeted us on the farm in Brady. Chasms between the Burks' simple words and my dark moods. Between their weathered perseverance and my daily worries. Now they were one—all rolled up into this man.

Simple pleasures, small victories. He won his first game as a coach on October 2, 1957. He wrote Mom that he would send her a press clipping. He described what he wore to the game, then summarized the game itself. His P.S. to her: the boys cheered for him on the bus ride home. Before that game, they hadn't scored the whole year. He said it touched him.

He would be dead in exactly two years and a day.

I threw down the letter. Pushed back my chair, stood up. Paced.

Wake up. Wake up to what's happening.

You dumb—

You poor, dumb—

You're going to die.

He never complained about his health, so he was fatigued for some time. Finally, he let my mother take him to the hospital. The doctors immediately put him in an iron lung.

A coach's wife baby-sat Tommy and me while Mom drove to the hospital to be with our father. Every day he looked worse. She had to signal to him in the iron lung, to communicate. His body kept withering.

Each day as she entered the hospital, she had a horrible, sinking fear. But she was afraid to think the worst. The more news they got from the doctors, though, the more they realized what was going to happen.

Finally, they talked about it. He told her he was sorry.

—A woman sat with me, Scotty. A sweet, sweet woman. Her husband was going to recover. I know now she was a Christian, because she always prayed for me, and she talked to me about Jesus. She tried to stay connected with me after Ronnie died, but after a while we just lost touch.

Two weeks, from diagnosis to death.

I was grateful someone was there to hold my mother's hand.

The students and faculty of West High School dedicate this yearbook page to the memory of Mr. Ronnie Witten Burk, who during the years 1957–1959 was a member of our teaching and coaching staff and who, during his tenure here, endeared himself in the hearts of all with whom he was associated. Even though he had left our school in the summer of 1959 to join the staff of the Channelview High School near Houston, Texas, his untimely death in early October of 1959 was deeply mourned by the teachers and students of our school. The memory of his fine char-acter, his pleasant personality, and his sincere devotion to the highest ideals of the teaching profession will always linger with us as a splen-did example of the best of America's young manhood. We are grateful

for having had the privilege to know and work with him, and rever-
ently join in seeking for ourselves, his dear wife, and his two little sons,
God's revelation of the lessons of which He would have us learn from
the one who has been so prematurely separated from us.

God's revelation of the lessons.

Is that what my father's death was? A lesson?

He'd been between jobs, between towns. He'd left West, but
hadn't really gotten started at Channelview. *Channelview*—just
a stone's throw from Houston. From Rice. From his dream.

Separate communities, book-ending his life. During those
last days, he was a part of neither. Was there anyone there,
besides us, to mourn him?

Read in sequence, his letters give a magical sweep to those two
years in his life—years when he was just getting started, looking out at the world in worry and wonder.

I had more questions for my mother. But she had fewer and
fewer answers.

"You have to remember something, honey," she finally said.
"I only knew him for less than three years."

23

I dialed Texas. Unsure of what I wanted, what to ask for.

Dad answered.

My voice cracked. I couldn't speak.

He hesitated—panicking, I could tell. Stalling, searching for Mom.

Maybe she wasn't around. Maybe she was in the background, motioning for him to stay on with me. Or maybe, somehow, my father heard my need.

Tommy's final months. I had blanked out almost everything. Now I wanted to know. I knew Dad always remembered details. Buzzy had inherited that from him.

He gave them to me, judiciously. As he talked, I remembered my own.

Phantom pains. The pain pills Tommy had to take. The horseshoe-shaped scar from his lung surgery, stretching from his chest to his back.

The rest came back to me. His agony, his vacant stares. His friends at school, asking about him. My answer: *Fine*.

—Did you still think he was going to be healed then?

—No. We knew. We just couldn't—

Dad gathered himself.

—We just couldn't let him go. Three days before he died, your mother and I asked the Lord to take him.

—Really?

I told him how relieved I'd been when they gave me the news.

He reflected on it for a minute.

—I couldn't act relieved, Scotty.

—Why not?

Now his voice cracked.

—People would have thought I didn't care.

Because he was only our stepfather.

The funeral.
    —It was a beautiful day, I remembered.
    —A Sunday, Dad said.
    —We came home, and the NBA Finals were on.
Something else, he reminded me.
    —It was Mother's Day.

Five men. One woman, at the center of us all.
    Two men came to her. Three came from her.
    Our mother, holding us together. Carrying one, sick and dying. Comforting one who had bloody hands. Buying shoes for another, to keep him running.

—We never made the trip to Houston, did we?
    —Yes, you did.
    —Buzzy and I?
    —Yes. Your mother wanted you to go at least one time. To see what it was like for Tommy, what his days were like down there. Maybe it was stupid of us, but we did it.
    —Are you sure we went?
    —Scotty, I remember where we stayed. I took you and Buzzy to a Holiday Inn, and your mother stayed at M. D. Anderson with Tommy. Don't you remember?
    I didn't.
    —What did we do?
    —She took Tommy to see *American Graffiti*. I took you boys over to Rice, to see the stadium. You don't remember any of that?

The medical bills—they must have been astronomical.

—Yeah, they were.

—How did they get paid?

—I don't know. They just did. The money always came in.

—When did we meet you, Dad?

—You mean . . .

—When Tommy and I first met you.

—I called your mother, and we all went on a date to the park. She and I, and you and Tommy.

—How old were we?

—You were in diapers. We hadn't been there five minutes when you'd filled them.

He laughed.

—You were screaming like a banshee. Meantime, Tommy runs off and jumps in a mud puddle.

I smiled.

—What happened then?

—What do you think happened? We cut everything short and went home.

Cut everything short.

—What an introduction, I said.

—Yeah, he said, his voice trailing off.

Mom called me a few days later. She wanted to tell me some things. Her voice trembled as she spoke:

—I know I built up Ronnie to you guys.

She had trouble speaking.

—I couldn't hide the fact from your dad . . . He lived in Ronnie's shadow for years.

She was silent for a moment.

—How could I do that to him, even though I couldn't—

She choked.

—I couldn't help it?

—Your Dad could have taken jobs where he worked on Saturdays. Jobs that paid more. But he wanted to be with his sons, to be at all your games.

I lingered on the phone. Wouldn't let her hang up. Finally—

—Mom.

—Yes?

—About Tommy.

—What about him?

—Those last weeks.

She waited for me.

—I didn't . . .

The phone shook in my hand.

—Yes, son?

—I didn't talk to him.

—I know it, Scotty. I know—

—He didn't look at me.

—Son—

—I didn't really know . . .

I brought my hand to my eyes.

A moment passed. Then—

—Let me tell you something, Scotty. He was in pain all that time. All the time. And he didn't want to be mean to you and Buzzy.

My whole body shook.

My brother.

—That's why, son.

That's why.

24

Sun. Dec. 7, 1997

 Dear Scotty and Joy,

 I think I will write all over this paper and forget margins, etc., and just put more words down. I have so much to write that I hardly know where to begin.

 First of all, Scotty, thank you for your really beautiful letter. I, especially, was so touched to realize what a difficult time it was for you and Tommy all those years. But also, what a blessing to know that you learned to love Robert, and I am so thankful for that. Tody and Jesse thought so much of Robert and appreciated all that he did for you boys. And to put it in true perspective, if Ronnie had lived, he would not have been perfect! No one is, not even those we may have held on a "mental pedestal"—am I making sense?

 I think so often of what I want to tell you—how much we love Patricia and what a difficult time it was when Ronnie was so suddenly taken away, leaving two little sons he was never to know. Then, when Tommy was so sick, and died, it was almost a repetition of Ronnie's death as far as the pain of it all—except that by then we had all grown a little closer to our Heavenly Father, and that helped in so many ways. My daddy never knew about Tommy—he grieved about Ronnie's death all the rest of his life, and I believe that his death from the heart attack was really caused by a broken heart, at least indirectly.

 Charles' son, Ronnie, is a freshman at Southwest Texas State University. He has a partial athletic scholarship (discus and shot put). I wish you could know him. He reminds me so much of his namesake— his quiet, sweet ways and thoughtfulness. He's a big boy—6 ft. and 210 lbs.—and it's all hard muscle!

 I hope both of you are well, and that your work is going well (I'm sure of it!). Keep us posted, and remember that we love you wherever you are—you're always close to us in our hearts.

 We love you, dearly,

 Aunt Louise

 (and Uncle Pinky)

Resurrections

For two years after he graduated, Buzzy strung along some jobs selling insurance. He had higher aims, but he wanted to keep a flexible schedule so he could go to pro training camps if he got invited. He'd had an informal tryout with the Packers over one spring break at Baylor and, later, a passing interest from the Bengals. His closest shot came the next year, when he spent a week at the Falcons' camp in Atlanta. He made it to the middle round of cuts before he was sent packing.

When the Cowboys were on a downward slide in the late 1980s, they held open tryouts for punters and placekickers at Texas Stadium. Buzzy and Cristal were living nearby at the time, and my brother decided he'd give it a final shot. Dozens of guys showed up, but only Buzz and two others got invitations to training camp. After a week or two, everybody was gone except Buzzy and the Cowboys' resident punter. Buzz knew he was probably being retained just to push the starter. That only made him more determined.

It came down to the last day. Finally, when the team roster was announced, Buzzy's name wasn't on it. As Dad might have said, he knew then it was time to hang 'em up.

Just before the season started, the NFL Players Union called a strike. The league owners didn't want to meet the union's demands, so they called in replacement players, or "scabs." These were made up mostly of the last guys in training camp to get cut. Buzzy got a call from the Cowboys.

Joy and I were dating at the time, and we saw him play in a couple of televised games, one of them a Monday Night Football broadcast. There he was, standing in the end zone of Texas Stadium, wearing the blue star on his helmet.

His string of luck ran out after three games, when the strike ended.

"Didn't mind the paychecks," he told me.

Tulsa World, "Sports Extra," October 1987:
Eight years ago, a tribute to Roger Staubach landed on the desk of Dallas sports writer Blackie Sherrod. It was flowery, even pretentious, with

phrases like "He was our Caesar, the man whom Cassius encountered. He doth bestride our narrow world like a Colossus" and, well, you get the idea.

But this tome was not written by some star-blinded groupie, or hero-worshipping adolescent. It was the work of a mother forever grateful for what one of life's heroes had done for her dying son.

Staubach, when quarterback of the Cowboys, befriended a fifteen-year-old boy named Tommy dying of osteogenic sarcoma. Bone cancer. He sent him tickets, gave him his private telephone number, told him to call any time. It made the inevitable easier.

The subject came up again this week, when the same mother wrote Sherrod again.

Tommy had been a tight end on his [ninth grade] football team. His younger brother specialized in kicking, and together they collected many a Punt, Pass & Kick trophy. In the summer Tommy built wooden goal posts and lined yard markers on the street for his brother's kicking targets. He barked at the lad through long hours of practice, driving him on.

"It became that kind of football summer for them," the mother wrote, "the days of Tony Franklin and Russell Erxleben—those fall seasons when the only game for Texas boys is football."

The cancer took Tommy's leg, but not his football. He pushed his younger brother harder still, venting his frustration while prodding the other boy to greater achievements.

And then Tommy died.

But his dream did not. The younger brother would not let it.

"After the grass had long grown over the tombstone engraved with a football," wrote the chronicler of life in Texas, "he kept punting.

"There are only 28 of them. In America. But Tommy's brother became one. He no longer punts past chalk marks on neighborhood streets. There is no voice yelling from the end of the block. He punts on artificial turf now."

Perhaps not for long. Buzzy Sawyer, an all-Southwest Conference punter at Baylor, punted last week for Dallas' replacement team. As soon as the strike is over, he'll probably be a civilian again. But he got his wish, for his dead brother, and, writes his mother, Pat Sawyer, "Call him a scab, or what you will."

25

My buddy Stu Lumpkins had come to Denver again, this time with a fellow lawyer named Bill. They'd just wrapped up a deposition and were looking for a good place to eat dinner. I drove them through the Cherry Creek area, where we passed Larry's Shoes.

"You've got Larry's Shoes in Denver?" Stu said. "I thought that was strictly a Fort Worth institution."

"Dad wants to go in there every time he and Mom come to town," I said. "He sent me the pair I've got on from Larry's in Fort Worth."

Bill was incredulous. "Your family gives you *shoes?*"

"Sure," I said. "And watches. Dad takes care to get you those two things."

And something else. We'd let our "adoption anniversary" lapse. Dad renewed it in 1992:

Dear Scotty,
I can't believe it's been 21 years since the day you were adopted. As I told you, I remember you and Tommy wearing your purple outfits to go to court, and afterwards we went to Brookside Inn to have lunch. You know, 21 years is a long time!
I tried to think of something appropriate to commemorate your 21 years as "Sawyer," and the only thing I could really think of was to get you a nice writing instrument. What more could a writer ask for than a Mont Blanc pen? So, in honor of our 21st anniversary, I want you to take this pen and write. I want you to be released to write, write, write! I know it's been a long time since you really wrote, and I know God gave you such a talent. Use this pen to become what He wanted you to be, and when you use it, think of October 22, 1971.
Love,
Dad

But I couldn't. Couldn't write.

Won't, a workshop leader said to our group. *There's a difference between can't and won't.* He echoed all the common wisdom on writing. *Writing is a choice, an act of volition. Nobody* can't *write.*

I'd been a professional editor for fifteen years. Magazines, journals, newsletters. Any writing I did came on the side—reviews, articles, a few lengthy essays.

"Isn't that writing?" a friend asked. She and her husband were sitting with us in a restaurant patio, sipping iced tea.

"I think of myself as an editor," I said.

"Why?" she asked.

"I don't know," I said. "Because I don't write."

"Why don't you?" her husband asked.

I really couldn't say.

"Why don't you think of yourself as a writer who makes your living as an editor?" he probed.

I thought about that one.

"Well, which do you think you are?" he asked.

They were honest questions. And these were good friends. I answered honestly.

"I guess I'm a writer."

"I've *never* heard you say that," my friend said. Yet he acted as if he'd known it all along.

"So," he asked, "what's holding you back?"

Joy and I were simply opening mail at the kitchen table. I dropped the letters and started crying.

—What is it? she asked.

I couldn't talk. I didn't think I knew.

I did.

—How can you put up with this?

—With what?

She waited patiently.

–The guilt.

I choked out the words:

–All the guilt that affects us. That I've dragged into ... What it does to us. What it keeps us from.

She was silent.

–How can you live with it?

She leaned forward. Her hand was on mine.

–I love you, she whispered. You and all your guilt.

That night, we were lying in bed when it started again. This time, I couldn't stop.

Joy seemed to know. She said nothing, but held me.

A long time passed.

Then, it came.

–I didn't want to steal from him.

She let a moment pass.

–Steal what?

I couldn't say it. Then it would be true–what I'd done to my brother. But it was true already.

I said it.

–*He* was the writer. *He* was the writer.

He had wanted life–real life, not movies. He'd wanted a real father, not just the idea of one. And he wanted to write–of experience, of friendship, of a girl, of the wide world, not just of inner demons. I could write of nothing else.

Yet I knew I could never do justice to my brother in words. To the feeling I'd had when I rubbed my hand over his crew cut. To seeing him catch passes from Darrell, kick field goals with Buzzy. To watching him walk steadily down the hallway with his friends, concealing his prosthesis. To sitting beside him, both of us wide-eyed and in pain, as brown blood covered his body.

I didn't want to diminish him. My brother had been cheap-
ened enough already. I couldn't let him twist in the wind before
the whole world.

The way God had let him.

Joy and I were at a writers conference in Grand Rapids, Michigan, a biannual gathering we never missed. One of the keynote
speakers was Elie Wiesel. I'd expected a somber evening, full
of deep counsel about taking life more seriously, exhortations
to treat every day as if it were our last. Wiesel was nothing like
this. He was full of humor and high spirits, telling anecdotes
with a refreshingly light air. He spoke of being a young, aspir-
ing writer, thrilled to meet Samuel Beckett, the playwright who
would help him get published. And he ended with humor by
wishing us all—a crowd of two thousand—publication and fame.

At one point he spoke of some of the differences between
the Christian and Jewish approaches to God. One such difference, he said, is illustrated in the biblical characters we seek to
emulate. Christians, for example, honor Noah, because of his
unquestioning obedience. When God gave this man the over-
whelming task of building a giant ark that would float when the
Flood came, Noah didn't bat an eye. Jews, on the other hand,
Wiesel said, revere Job. Here was the man who asked, "Why?"
Who, when he'd lost everything, pointed a questioning finger
at God, cried out at him, and was rewarded for it.

I was sitting on our front porch on a Saturday morning when a
friend stopped by, a new father strolling his baby son. I decided
to walk with them to the park, a few blocks down the street.

My friend is a Christian. Along the way, I asked him about the
changes he'd experienced since having a child. He spoke of how
much more responsibility he felt—how he would do anything to
protect his son from harm. He'd never known this impulse existed
in him, he said, before he and his wife had this son.

"Let me ask you something," I said. "When you think of God as a father, do you ever think of what he did to his children at the Red Sea?"

He asked what I meant.

"I mean, letting the Israelites sit there as Pharaoh roared down on them. Letting them dangle, scared, in front of the enemy until the very last minute. And then getting them out of there, just in time. When all along he could have delivered them gently and peacefully, the day before."

My friend was silent.

I wasn't finished. "Would you do that to your son? Is that how you'd teach him you'd always be faithful to him?"

But that wasn't what God had done with our family, I thought. He'd let us stand at the Red Sea. And he'd let Pharaoh get there.

I'd driven south to Colorado Springs to have dinner with a good friend. We hadn't met for a while, and his expression told me he wasn't quite ready when I started unloading. I told this guy everything that was boiling in my soul—about Tommy's last few months. About my empty day on a hilltop in Los Angeles. About doubt, fear, unbelief.

"What did you expect to hear that day?" my friend asked.

In L.A.?

"Yes."

I didn't know.

"Why don't you think God spoke to you?"

I shrugged.

"What did you think at the time?"

I didn't think anything. I didn't want to know.

"Why not?"

Who'd want to know the reason why God doesn't talk to them?

He laughed, nodding.

"But you were lost," he said.

And?

"When a sheep gets lost, Jesus goes after it." He stated it as a fact.

A nice enough thought, I told myself.

"That's what he does," he added. "He picks it up, puts it on his shoulders, and brings it home."

My friend could see my resistance. He pointed out something else. "I see you doing all these things to try to get to God. Why don't you let him come and get you?"

I was barely able to stay on the road. The wheel shook from my trembling hands. My shoulders were heaving, heaving with lostness.

Come and get me, Jesus. Please, come and get me.

seven

Cathedrals

People say making movies isn't a cure for cancer. I disagree; filmmaking is a cure. It gives you a reason for living. When my son died, on the third day I was devastated, I didn't know what to do with myself. I went to see *Orlando*. It was so beautiful. This earth can be transformed. There are moments of extreme wonder . . . and that's all worth living for.

—Jane Campion

26

MY COUSIN MARTHA HAD CALLED MOM—AUNT LOUISE'S EIGHT-ieth birthday was coming up. The kids were going to hold a reception for her the following weekend in Dublin, Texas, where she and Uncle Pinky had moved.

As Mom cradled the phone, she glanced at Dad. He could tell what the conversation was about. He motioned for her to get directions.

"We're having people write letters to Mother in her honor," Martha said. "Please let Scotty and Buzzy know about it. I've seen Mother read Scotty's letters. She reads them over and over."

Remembering.
  Staring at the present, while looking into the past.
  Wondering.

Mom wrote to us the day before she and Dad drove to Dublin:

I'd like to see everyone again, but I always experience such bittersweet-ness when I'm around the Burks. So much floods old memories, digs them up, calls them to the surface with the pain I'd thought I'd forgot-ten forever, but that part of Texas, Ronnie's relatives, their physical pres-ence, their sounds, just how they move and laugh, their subtle quiet humor, their soft way of speaking, their memories of him, all exhume that gut-stabbing recollection I thought was eternally buried, exhumed only when I opted to deliberately feel loss and deep, deep pain.

Before she retired from teaching, Mom was honored by the State of Texas as one of the ten outstanding teachers. She and Dad attended a ceremony in Austin, where she was fêted along with nine of her peers from across the state.

When she finally did retire, in 1998, her school notified many of her former students beforehand about the event. They happily sent in letters of tribute. The messages came from Berkeley, Cambridge, Chicago, and New York, as well as Wax-ahachie, Burleson, Joshua, Crowley—and Midlothian.

Joy and I had spent a long weekend with my parents at their home near Fort Worth. We had one day of vacation remaining before we returned to Denver.

We'd spent most of our time lounging around the house, a one-story ranch that Dad and Mom had moved into after Buzzy left for A&M. When they first moved in, the house stood naked-looking on the hilltop, with a lone tree—a tall post oak—in the front yard. Aside from that, the yards were bare of foliage. Not surprisingly, eighteen years later the house stood out on their block as a jungle of gardens, hedges, and flower beds. They'd put a birdbath in the backyard, and later a bubbling fountain. One summer Buzzy built a small fence for them around the patio and painted it white. Dad added an arched gateway. And there were the ever-present hummingbird feeders. Every morning, my parents said, they watched the speedy hummers feeding as they had their coffee.

Before our visit, I'd talked with Mom about the four of us possibly spending a day in Waxahachie. I also asked if she and Dad would mind not seeing anyone while we were there. I just wanted us to be together as a family for the day, drinking in some memories. "Sure," she'd answered.

Now, we'd just finished dinner and sat poking around the table.

"Waxahachie tomorrow?" Mom asked.

"Great," I said.

The route that runs between Fort Worth and Waxahachie—U.S. Highway 287—runs southeast to northwest. If you're driving from Waxahachie and follow the highway northwestward, you'll reach Fort Worth in forty-five minutes. If you follow it for another fourteen hours or so, you'll end up on Federal Boulevard in Denver—a half block from Joy's and my first home there.

We'd planned only three destinations in Waxahachie—an antique store my parents wanted us to see, a dress shop Mom wanted to show Joy, and a café for lunch. All three places were downtown, near the square.

We were approaching the city limit west of town when Mom said, "Slow down, Robert."

"I know, I know," he said.

We were nearing Hilltop Cemetery, on the right. It was where Tommy was buried.

I hadn't expected it. My parents had never initiated any formal remembrances. They must have sensed what I might've wanted.

Dad turned right, onto the gravel driveway and under the wrought-iron arch. He drove along the narrow, two-track path up the hill. We passed the familiar cedars on the left, then stopped. There it was, on the left—the gray-colored marker raised just above the ground, with a red football etched on it. And the dates: July 14, 1958–May 9, 1974. The name, Thomas Witten Sawyer, with his football number, 80, and the name everyone knew him by, in quotation marks: "Tommy." Next to it was our cousin Robbie's marker.

"Buzzy ran in a track meet that day," Mom reminded us. She started to cry. "Remember, Scotty?"

Dad put his arm around Mom.

I thought of Darrell Wilson. I wondered if he'd been out here lately. I knew he drove by here, on the way to his parents' house from his own home in Arlington. I wondered if he ever thought about that day, May 9, as he passed the cemetery—if he'd felt lost, as I had, or if he'd been able to draw meaning from his loss.

Joy squeezed my hand.

Dad drove straight to the other cemetery. We weren't going to spare any of our mourning. This one was in the middle of town, next to the high school baseball park. Dad turned right off of Main Street and onto the narrow lane leading to the cemetery. The grounds sit under vast, leafy oak trees which, on overcast days, make the cemetery look like a haunted forest.

Just inside the entrance, Dad took a quick right onto the narrow gravel drive. He drove for maybe a hundred feet and stopped. The stones were on the left.

I realized only then that I'd never seen Poppy and Ween's gravestones. I hadn't come back for either of their funerals. Dad had written me letters in Los Angeles when they were sick. He began them with amusing observations from home, burying the hard news about his parents in the third paragraph or so. Even then, he soft-pedaled it. Buzzy later told me that Dad had lost a startling amount of weight during that time, withering in the weeks after his parents' deaths.

We stepped out of the car. As we read the inscriptions and stood next to each other in silence, I imagined my father standing over his parents' graves—Poppy and Ween, dying only a few months apart—as they were laid in the ground. I also imagined Mom and Buzzy there with him, and wondered if they'd cried.

A huge chasm opened within me. Now I would remember where they are.

We stood on the sidewalk a block from the courthouse square. Dad and I cupped our hands around our eyes, trying to peer into the space once occupied by Morris Head's Men's Shop. He had taken me there as a senior, to get fitted for my first suit—a silvery-blue three-piece I'd wanted, which lasted through college. I reminded Dad of this, as Mom and Joy nosed around the dress shop nearby. I was feeling wistful.

"Makes you wonder if you could ever move back here," I said.

Dad was startled. "Oh, Scotty, how could you ever consider that? It depresses me to be back here."

"Really?"

His reaction caught me off guard. Twenty years earlier, he might have lit up a Kool. Now he stuffed his hands in his pockets and rocked back and forth on his heels.

"Sure," he said. "This is where everything bad happened."

Burying Tommy. Burying Ween and Poppy.

I realized he was speaking of his life—not Mom's, not mine, not our family's. *His.*

And I saw that I'd missed a significant part of it. That's the way it had always been, though—our needs first, then his. We'd rarely ever gotten around to his.

We were back on U.S. 287, heading home on the two-lane stretch of green between Waxahachie and Midlothian. We were approaching a hill, an upward slope, when I noticed the back of Dad's neck—a crossing of lines, with white fuzz. I had a flash of memory. I saw again the weathered neck of Grandjesse.

Now I saw two men who'd walked the same path. Who'd each had to ask God, in his own way, "Why did you take my son?" Who'd learned to rise up early to start for their destinations, because something unexpected could happen on the way. Who'd had to persevere, always—to keep walking, keep moving, keep living—because others depended on it.

And I remembered important words:

On becoming a man, there are responsibilities that you will for the first time inherit. The ability to face disappointment, to feel compassion for those less fortunate than you, to help those weaker than you, to show kindness and understanding when it seems almost impossible.

I thought of the revived puppy, King—surely twice dead now, but alive to me back then more than any other living thing. His sibling had died, its body damaged irreversibly. And though King had seemed dead at the time, he had lived. He'd been brought to life as if by magic—by a stranger, no less, someone who hadn't had to care, but who had. Whose strong hands pumped life into his limp body.

Daddy Robert—my second father. My earthly father. He brought things to life with his hands. He brought me to life. And he lay my brother, his son, in the ground with a father's care and love.

Dad and I both had been second.

We had this in common as well: we were left behind. Asked to wither over the dead. To carry on, to limp. To face anxieties, worries, struggles, bills, maybe more cancer. To go to church, to pray, to wonder in our thousand doubting moments if we're ever heard.

To live.

When we got home, the pump had been primed. Dad started the grill, while Mom, Joy, and I hauled in box after box from the garage. We sat at the kitchen table sorting through everything.

Pictures of Tommy and me in black and white—babies, walking gingerly in the snow, with Mom and Aunt Dianne on either side of us. A picture of Daddy Robert in the backyard, shirtless, holding Clyde as a puppy. We shuffled through the photos like playing cards, shoving them to each other with little more than a grunt. Mom to Joy: pictures of me at various stages. Me to Joy: comical shots of my brothers and me in bell-bottoms, wide ties, high-water pants. Joy to me: images of my older brother, whom she'd never known.

Mom slid a picture toward me. It was a shot of Buzzy and me. For some reason, the picture was taken in black and white. We were standing next to each other in the backyard, each holding a basketball. It was winter, and the tree limbs were bare. It was a wide shot, with a lot of space on either side of us.

"That was during Tommy's chemo," Mom said.

Buzzy and I both wore jeans and mock football jerseys, with our shirttails hanging out, and long underwear with the sleeves showing. It was what we wore to school during those days. My hair had gotten long, longer than it had ever been. Buzzy's bangs were combed straight down, covering his eyebrows, almost down over his eyes.

"I can't stand to look at that picture," Mom said.

I came across a paper plate, ridged on the edges, with a note written in green ink. Dad had left it for Mom before leaving one morning. It was signed with the closing, "21"–their mysterious secret code, which they'd kept sacred, between themselves.

A statistic: Eighty percent of all couples who lose a child to death end in divorce.

I carried the last box back out to the garage.

"Hey, Scotty," Dad said, meaning to stop me. He'd picked up some item from the table, and stuffed it into the top of the box I was carrying. He turned back to the dishes–then he stopped in his tracks, snapping his fingers and pivoting, the way he does when he suddenly remembers something.

"You know, your father–," he began.

He was speaking of Ronnie.

My father?

Dad kept talking, matter-of-factly. I didn't hear another word.

I don't want to hear you saying this. You don't understand.

I don't remember what he said. Just those two words– *Your father.* From him.

It was his grief.

Grief does odd things to people.

That night, as Joy and Mom gathered some mementos for us to pack, Dad and I found ourselves standing in the small dressing room between their bedroom and bathroom. It had been a good day, a full day in every sense. Now we chatted casually as he rifled through some jewelry drawers, looking for a tie tack or something.

He came across something in a drawer. It stopped him in mid-sentence. He slowly lifted a ring—Ronnie's college ring.

We gazed at it in his palm. It looked odd cupped in Dad's thick hand. He clearly didn't know what it was doing there. I didn't either.

He reached back into the drawer, scrabbled around and found the other one—the Brady High School ring.

He held them out to me.

"Do you want to take these with you?" he asked.

I looked down at them.

"No," I said. "You keep them for me."

27

I had seen Dad change, ever so subtly, when Buzzy's first daughter, Whitten, was born. She was the first grandchild, and she came out unmistakably a Sawyer—round eyes, round nose, round head, round ears. In fact, she looked just like *Dad*.

That was the first time I thought of our family's heritage—our future memory—as being that of a Sawyer, and not a Burk or Meadows. Overnight, I saw my father, and us, differently. Dad, a patriarch.

Joy and I were on our way to Houston, to visit Buzzy and Cristal and their two daughters. As we sat in the airport, waiting to board our plane, I scanned the gate area absently. Standing directly in front of us was a group of a dozen or so people. It was clearly an extended family, with one group saying goodbye to their departing relatives.

They were all standing in an informal circle, the men talking to one another, the women doing the same. The young kids, cousins probably, giggled and punched each other, playing tag and darting between the adults.

Three men stood on the fringe of the circle, rubbing their beards and shifting their weight from side to side. They each shared the same features—same stocky build, same squinty eyes. It was clear they were brothers.

Their gazes meandered as they grinned and nodded, talking of nothing more, probably, than the weather or carburetors. Three men in middle age—complacently taking in the wonder of how fast each other's children had grown, how their own bellies had sprouted spare tires, how the other two were beginning to look and act like their dad. Each enjoying the midlife fruit of having been a sibling for forty-some-odd years. Stretching out a momentary goodbye.

Our nieces, Whitten and Faith, were three and two. Mom and Dad said they reminded them of Tommy and me all over again—one always provoking the other, angling for position.

Tonight the girls were "helping" Joy and Cristal to make dinner. Buzz pulled into the driveway in their Honda Passport, home from work.

"Daddy's home," Cristal announced.

The girls rushed to the door—Whitten pushing aside her younger sister, Faith crying, "No, me, me."

"Whitten, let Faith stand by the door with you," Cristal commanded.

Whitten glanced at me, grinning mischievously. She wanted me to know that Buzzy was *her* daddy, even if her sister tried to claim him too.

The girls peered through the glass, watching their father step out of the vehicle with his briefcase. When he came through the kitchen door, he was smiling, ready for them. They leaped on him like monkeys, each clutching a leg, laughing, "Daddy, Daddy."

Buzz walked across the kitchen stiff-legged, like Frankenstein, his briefcase still in his hand. I followed him into the girls' bedroom, his daughters still clutching him. He wrestled them off, squealing, and onto the bed.

I glimpsed a familiar picture on the girls' bedroom wall. I looked closer.

"That's Uncle Tommy," Whitten instructed me.

Tommy.

The picture seemed out of place. An image of sadness, sorrow.

"That's right, Whitten," Buzzy said. "Can you tell Uncle Scotty who Uncle Tommy was?"

"Brother," she said shyly.

When Buzzy had changed clothes, he motioned to me quietly. Then he announced to Cristal, "Hey, we're going to take a walk before dinner. We can take the girls."

We strolled around the block of their neighborhood, letting the girls lead us. "Follow me, Uncle Scotty," Whitten beckoned.

My little brother had grown into a father while I wasn't looking. The brother I'd seen run in a track meet the day our older brother died—running and winning, never stopping after that. Never looking back, because, as he still says, life's too short. He'd poured his all into everything—into football, his M.B.A., his consulting work; into making a home with Cristal, making a family. Making a future.

"Do you remember those forts you used to draw?" he said. He recalled them as if he'd just seen them. "Those things were amazing. All the lines, the details—*in ink*. I look back and wonder how you did them."

A long time ago.

Then, out of the blue, he said something about Daddy Ronnie. He used those words—

"—Daddy Ronnie—"

—and it took me off guard. He was talking about territory that had always been strictly mine—mine and Tommy's.

Yes—Buzzy's *Daddy Ronnie*. Our *Daddy Ronnie*.

He was full of surprises that evening. "You know," he said, "if you or I don't have any boys, it's the end of the Sawyer line."

I never thought such things crossed Buzzy's mind. They simply hadn't been a topic in our family.

"I've thought about it," I said. "I guess there's Stevie." I was referring to Dad's nephew, in Waxahachie. We hadn't seen him since high school.

"That's true."

"You realize there won't be any more Burks," I said.

This gave Buzz pause. He processed it—Ronnie and Tommy, gone. And now me, a Sawyer.

"I guess you're right," he said thoughtfully.

"Well, there's Laney," I said. Daddy Ronnie's nephew. I'd only met him once, years before on the farm.

"And there's a Ronnie, at least," Buzzy added. "Ronnie Porter." Charles's son.

"Yeah," I said.

We left it at that.

On Sunday morning, Buzzy and Cristal introduced us to their Sunday school class. Everyone commented on the resemblance between Buzz and me. "Nobody would ever guess you're brothers," someone joked.

They were right. Nobody would have guessed it—at one time, in another place. When we were known as half brothers.

But as Solomon knew, you can't cut someone in half.

My dreams of Tommy had become infrequent. Now they came only every few years. The same old dynamics were always at work—he was still distracted, talking to someone else, paying attention to something other than to me.

But the dreams also had become progressive over the years. Each time, I recognized earlier that I was only dreaming, and I wasn't as disappointed when I woke.

Finally, a few years ago, I was no longer fooled at all. I realized as the dream began what was happening. So I sat back and observed my brother. In that dream, he softened toward me and even began talking with me. I just listened to him. But after a while, I couldn't contain it any longer. I reached out and hugged him. He smiled

I haven't seen him since.

I also connected with my first father one final time.

I was sitting in a coffee shop, scribbling some notes. And then, he was there—sitting casually across the table from me. Having a cup of coffee. Smiling.

The box from Aunt Louise. Same pumping of the heart . . .

I sat looking at him, imagining him. Envisioning him in work clothes, having come from some summer odd job during his time off from coaching. Quietly sipping his coffee—from the saucer, perhaps, as Grandjesse had done. Catching up on me, yet not saying a word.

I eyed him slowly, deliberately, taking him in once more—his lanky build, his posture like mine, his face rounder and puffier with age. His eyes wrinkled, his hair now gray.

I slid back in my chair. This time, I had no questions for him, I realized. Instead, my mind drifted past him, to what was ahead of me that day. Then I thought of the next day, and the day after that, and the one after that.

Not of things on a list. Of simply *things in a day*.

All the while, imagining a day to come.

28

It was the morning of Good Friday 1999. Joy had narrowly missed getting caught in the blizzard that hit the night before. She'd been driving to Colorado Springs when it started—on her way to spend the night with a small gathering of women. They were going to spend the next morning in prayer, focusing on the day's significance.

We'd planned for Joy to drive home on Friday afternoon, so we could attend a Good Friday service at an Episcopal church that evening. We'd made it a tradition. Each year, the entire service consisted of the cathedral choir singing the passion from John's gospel. Our Lord's words.

Had become our words.

Now she called me from Colorado Springs.

"We're all holed up at Chuck and Katie's," she said. "I tried to get through on I-25, but I had to turn around at Monument. They closed everything down."

I heard laughter behind her.

"I think that's *The Princess Bride,*" Joy said. "They've got a pile of videos, and we're shutting ourselves in."

I lined up some pens before me on the kitchen table.

"Well, don't try driving for a while," I said.

Come to me, now.

"You know I'm not going to drive in this," she said.

"Call me later, if you want to."

Don't hang up.

She laughed. "You know I'm going to call you, love. I'm calling you *now*. You sound like you're in a hurry to get off the phone."

I let a brief silence fall.

"What are you going to do?" Joy asked.

"I don't know."

It kicked in even before I hung up the phone. The list.
  Projects, chores, tasks, letters. The list, the list, the list.
  A full day ahead, and a full list.
  Stomach churning.
  Hands rubbing. Wringing.
  His day—a holy day.
  Holy? I'm *alone.* Is that holy?

Flip open to the list. Items on lines, lines, lines, lines, lines of lists.
  Note, fill, erase. Note, erase. Guardian of the lines. Organizing meaning from nothing. Pushing back chaos.

You took her from me today. On your *holy day.*
  Familiarity.
  Impermanent.

Churning.
  Good Friday.
  Lord, every time you come, you bring sadness with your joy.

Evening cathedral service, 7:00.
  Okay.
  Hands rubbing, wringing. Wringing, wringing.
  What now? Right *now?*

How do you rearrange lines—organize them, structure them, rely on them—when there are no more lines before you?

Movie listings.

The old vice.
Line upon line of show times.
Something near the cathedral ...
The Esquire, on Downing.
Central Station. 4:30. Brazilian movie.

—A few hours' escape, before coming to meet you, God.

---◁◇▷---

AN ORPHANED YOUNG BOY in Rio is searching for his father. The boy's name is Joshua. He somehow convinces a dour old woman to accompany him to a rural town, where he believes his father lives. They begin the trip by bus, a journey of several days.

Along the way, the woman reveals that she too had been abandoned by her father when she was a child.

Come and get us, Jesus.

When the pair arrive in the remote town, they receive bad news. Joshua's father doesn't live there after all.

Joshua begins to lose hope. But then a smiling young man appears, offering to help them. As it turns out, the young man—Isaiah—is Joshua's half-brother. Their father indeed had been in the town, Isaiah says. But he left a few years earlier to find work, promising to return.

Now Isaiah leads the pair to his home. He introduces them to his brother, Moses, a somber young man. The brothers are a study in contrasts: Isaiah—always smiling, always encouraging, ever hopeful. Moses—the eternal skeptic, his glass forever half empty.

Isaiah—encouraging voice of hope.
   Moses—harsh tongue of the law.

As Isaiah mentions their father's promise to return, he is hopeful.
Moses cannot believe it.

Isaiah—prophesying to a destitute people. A voice crying out in the Old Testament wilderness, pointing the way to the New. Wrestling with human reality, as Jacob did, to obtain a future hope.

Moses—pointing downward to the cracked earth, his temper flaring. Beating the people's heads with stone tablets, as John Bunyan caricatured him.

The boys' father had sent them a letter months before, but they're illiterate. They ask the old woman to read the letter to them. She unfolds the message.

The father writes of his great love for his sons, and of his intention to return and unite them all.

Isaiah begins to cry.

The old woman looks up from the letter. She glances at Joshua, then continues to read: "And I can't wait to meet Joshua."

Joshua—one who will be delivered. One to be led into the promised land.

Joshua looks at her skeptically. Life has taught him to doubt.

A ringing sound of old words:
    Doubt, fear, unbelief. The enemies of your faith.

The old woman continues reading, down to the end.
    "I'm coming back," their father, Jesús, writes. "Wait for me."
    Isaiah looks up hopefully, his eyes wet.

Cathedrals

"He'll be back," he says.
"No, he won't," Moses states.
Young Joshua speaks up.
"Yes, he will," he says. "One day."

As the old woman finishes reading the letter, young Joshua's eyes are filled with longing. "Did he really mention me?" he asks.

He'd learned to doubt. But he had never lost hope. He always had both.

Moses and Isaiah.
    Twin prophets in my heart.

The old woman is on the bus now, returning to Rio. Joshua has stayed behind with his brothers. She begins a letter to the boy:
    "You were right. Your father will come back. And he surely is all you say he is."
    She finishes the letter—and the movie ends—with these vulnerable words:
    "I long for my father.
    "I long for everything."

Yes. Yes, I do.
    For an impossible family. An impossible reconciliation, in an impossible world.
    Where God has yet made all things possible.

And hope does not disappoint.

———————————— ◄◊► ————————————

THE SNOW HAD PILED a good six inches on my car. It stood high on the roof like a white fez, on the hood and trunk like shoulder pads. I brushed it from the windshield and rear window, and ducked inside the car. I started the engine and sat waiting for it to warm.

As the wipers cleared off the remaining snow, I saw that the sun had broken through. Yet, oddly, the snow continued to fall. It was one of those strange moments when both happen at once.

Good Friday.

The drive to the cathedral was slow, full of starts and stops. Cars sliding slowly, comically, down an incline, stranding themselves at the curb. I drove cautiously, eyeing the harmless mishaps, ready to help if needed.

I was going to a reunion. I would see a shepherd lift the cup of grace—a cup of blood—and extend it to a lengthening line ahead of me. A line of pilgrims, aliens, refugees, mothers and daughters, fathers and sons, all who seek.

And I would meet a Father there.

One who'd come to me today, like a faithful shepherd. Who'd found me in the darkened theater of my fears, and spoke hope to my longing, love to my loss. One who'd made my doubt a gift. Who'd turned my unbelief into a blessing. Who'd urged me through every misgiving about Him, "Seek, and you will find—*Me.*"

A Father whose warm hand had held my mother's, as her husband lay dying. Whose unseen hand had lifted my dying brother's eyes to his first sight of eternity. A shepherd who came and got me, through an earthly father's thick, strong hands— hands that had carried me, blessed me, commissioned me.

Cathedrals

A Father whose own words of comfort I would soon recite gladly, alongside other pilgrims—words unfettered by law, unaccusing in spirit, yet high and holy nonetheless. Words about his presence here and now, yet also there and then.
One day.

Will I see my earthly fathers embrace then? Perhaps I will.
Perhaps I have.

A serendipitous light that comes to us. Light that at first seems blindingly cruel, yet eventually shines into every darkened corner the hope of things to come.
Death—a curse. Yes.
A gift?
Yes.

Even death could not hold Him.

Snow falling like grace. Wipers moving in unison against the storm, brushing aside every wet drop. On my way from and to my epiphany—waiting for my Joy, longing for everything, on the way to my Father's house.

In the days of the voice of the seventh angel, when he shall begin to sound, the mystery of God should be finished . . .

—Revelation 10:7

In loving memory

Thomas Witten Burk Sawyer

Ronnie Witten Burk

Jesse Gross Burk

Clara Elizabeth Pennington Burk

Lester Thomas Burk

Robert Dean Forrester

Abby Lois Croom Meadows

William James Sawyer

Edna Halloween Price Sawyer

William Dudley Sawyer

Acknowledgments

I AM THANKFUL TO JESUS CHRIST, THE LORD—WHO ENDOWS every gift, painful and joyous, and whose love has given our family its story and watched over it faithfully.

I am indebted to my family: My father and mother, Charles Robert and Tommie Patricia Sawyer, and my brothers, Thomas Witten Burk Sawyer and Robert Meade Sawyer—Buzzy. I haven't presumed to speak for my family in this book, yet their gracious permission and love have allowed my words about us to be printed here. In the judgment of Mark Twain, "Life does not consist mainly—or even largely—of facts and happenings. It consists mainly of the storm of thoughts that is forever blowing through one's head." My thanks to my beloved parents and brothers, for allowing my personal storms to blow here.

To my invaluable writer friends, professionals in every sense of the word, for their insights, encouragement, and enduring friendship: most especially, my wife, Joy Sawyer—the gentle midwife who urged me at every stage to keep pushing; the discerning eyes who saw what was needed when I was blind; the compassionate angel on my shoulder who breathed love into every line. Enough can never be said about her contribution to the shape and content of this book. Also, to John Wilson, Stuart

C. Hancock, and Anton Marco—understanding friends whose own work and exhorting words always raise the bar; and to Chris Layne and Mark Miller, for their priceless friendship and encouragement in the task.

To the publications, organizations, and professionals who, at various times, helped give life to portions of this book: The 63rd Street Y Writers Workshops in New York; Lighthouse Writers of Denver; *Inklings* magazine; *Mars Hill Review; Image*'s Glen Workshops, in particular the generosity of Dan Wakefield; *Christianity and the Arts;* and Ad Lib Artists Retreats.

To my mentors and guides: especially my mother, Patricia Sawyer, whose influence cannot be measured, and my god-mother, Dr. Cleta M. Jones. Also, to Evelyn Berryman, Vicki Klaras, John V. Lawing Jr., Dr. Terry Lindvall, Carol M. Det-toni, S. Rickly Christian, and Dr. Maurice R. Irvin.

For crucial and lasting personal inspiration: Brent Curtis, whose memory and legacy broaden continually.

To the admired authors and artists whose works and words influenced this book directly: Jill Ker Conway, Diane Glancy, Tim Winton, Mike Nichols, Paul Schrader, Tim O'Brien, Ron Hansen, John Irving, Roy Blount Jr. Also, to Kathryn Black, author of the thoughtful and thorough book *In the Shadow of Polio: A Personal and Social History* (Addison-Wesley). And special thanks to Mr. Blount—for the Steelers signed football, and the lengths he went to get it, when it counted.

For championing this book: John Sloan, an enormously gifted, visionary, and sure-handed editor, with whom I discovered more than one sacred bond; and the devoted team at Zondervan Publishing House—John Topliff, Bob Hudson, Holli Leegwater, Megan Rowden, Emily Klotz, Sam Hooks, Greg Stielstra, Robin Welsh, Jessica Westra, Linda Palmer, Bob Hartig, Melissa Elenbaas, Stan Gundry, and many others, including the gracious Yanceys, who provided the introductions.

Most of all, to Joy, my most precious gift, who has always helped me to see clearly the most important things. Your love

Acknowledgments

and wisdom have shaped every line of this book, as well as everything in between. "... God's gifts put man's best dreams to shame."—E.B.B.

Credits

My gratitude to the members of my family—ROBERT AND Patricia Sawyer, Louise Porter, my late father, Ronnie Burk, and my late brother, Tommy Sawyer—for the honor of publishing their letters here.

My thanks also to the publications that have allowed me to quote them here:

"Playing With Heart," Randy Krehbiel, "Sports Extra," Tulsa *World,* October 10, 1987. Used by permission.

"The New Rebel Cry: Jesus is Coming!", *Time,* June 21, 1971, p. 56. Used by permission.

Kathleen Murphy, "Jane Campion's Passage to India," *Film Comment,* January-February 2000, p. 30. Used by permission.

We want to hear from you. Please send your comments about this
book to us in care of the address below. Thank you.

ZondervanPublishingHouse
Grand Rapids, Michigan 49530
http://www.zondervan.com